Highways of the West

America's Loneliest Road

U.S. 50 and the Lincoln Highway in Nevada

Stephen H. Provost

AMERICA'S LONELIEST ROAD

All material © 2022 Stephen H. Provost
Cover concept and design: Stephen H. Provost
Cover photograph: Stephen H. Provost
Back cover: Stephen H. Provost
All contemporary photographs © 2018-2022 Stephen H. Provost
Historical images are in the public domain, except where noted

No part of this book may be reproduced, or stored in a retrieval system, or transmitted in any form or by any means, electronic, mechanical, photocopying, recording, or otherwise, without the express written permission of the publisher.

Dragon Crown Books 2022

All rights reserved.

ISBN: 978-1-949971-29-3

Acknowledgments

Thanks to the Churchill County Museum, Eureka Sentinel Museum, East Ely Depot Museum, Nevada Department of Transportation, Russell Rein, University of Michigan Special Collections Research Center, and University of Nevada, Reno Special Collections and University Archives Department for use of their photographs. Special thanks to Brian Suen and the Lincoln Highway Association of Nevada for their vital role in providing and procuring historical illustrations for this work. Particular gratitude to Sharon Stora for her invaluable service as research assistant, consultant, pathfinder, and proofreader for this project.

STEPHEN H. PROVOST

More Reading

Contents

Lonely Beginnings	7
Utah State Line to Ely	19
Ely to Eureka	59
Eureka to Austin	101
Austin to Fallon	123
Fallon to Carson City	163
The Donner Route	165
The Pioneer Route	215
Carson City to Tahoe	253
Highway Timeline	277

Front cover photo by Stephen H. Provost
Old U.S. 50 near Carroll Summit, 2022

Back cover photo by Stephen H. Provost:
Replica Lincoln Highway marker between Austin and Eureka, 2022

America's Loneliest Road

Signs marking the Lincoln Highway are placed in Ely. *E. Holden Photo Album from the collection of Leon Schegg*

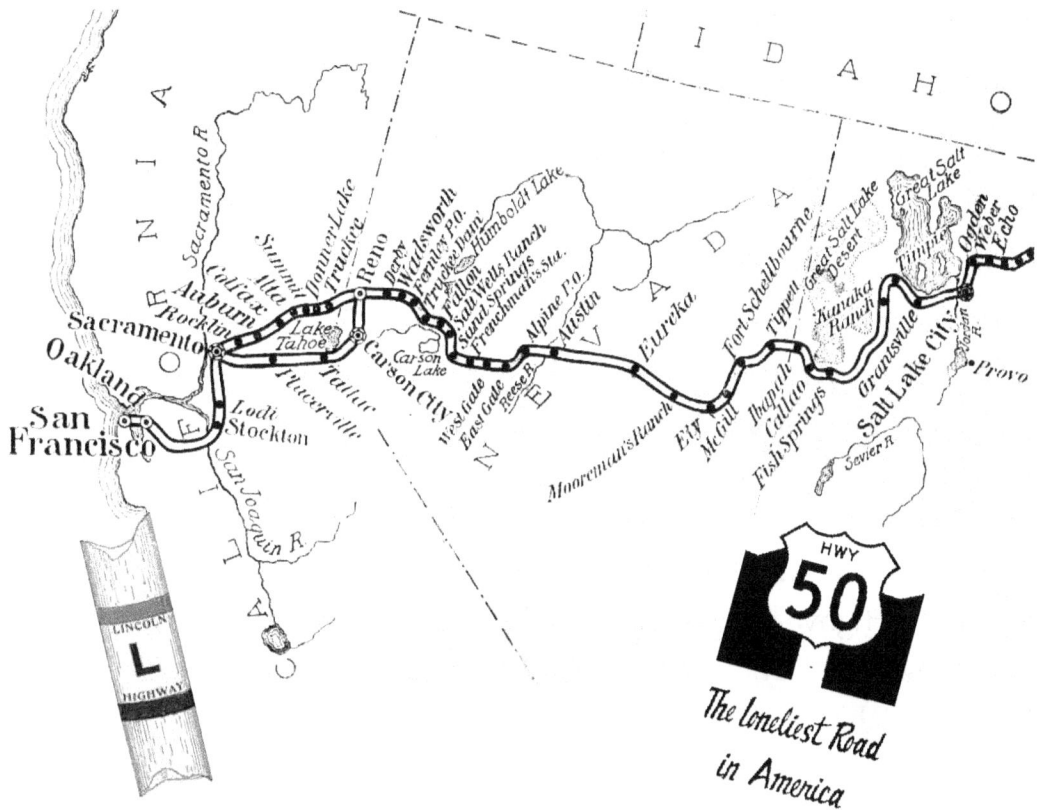

Lonely Beginnings

U.S. Highway 50 in Nevada has been called "The Loneliest Road in America" since 1986. It came courtesy of a *Life* writer, who bestowed that title upon it in the magazine's July edition, and it stuck.

To be certain, there are other lonely stretches of highway. Anyone who's driven old Route 66 through the Mojave Desert can testify to that. But it's hard to argue that band of asphalt from the Utah state line to Lake Tahoe is unworthy of the title. For vast distances, it extends outward toward the horizon in an unbroken line, attended only by sagebrush and empty spaces.

The high desert of eastern Nevada is, populated mostly with wild horses, antelopes, and jackrabbits. If you time your trip right, you may see vast numbers of Mormon crickets crossing the road near Austin, around the center of the state, or a herd of burros around Hickison Summit. But when it comes to human beings, they're few and far between.

It's 77 miles from Ely to Eureka, and 70 miles more from Eureka to Austin along the road, with virtually no sign of human habitation in between. The closest thing you're likely to come across is a water tank bearing the words "Nowhere, Nevada" or stone ruins abandoned more than a century ago by miners who moved on to the next big boom, even as they grew weary of the hard living and isolation.

Still, a road was needed to get from one more habitable place to another, and U.S. 50 filled the bill.

Most of its course through Nevada started out as the Overland Trail: the route taken by the Pony Express riders in 1861. Then, in 1913, that trail formed the basis for the Lincoln Highway (see map, previous page), the first road to span the continent. Unlike today's government-funded roads, the Lincoln Highway was paid for entirely through private funds from companies like Willys-Overland, which contributed $25,000, and General Motors, which forked over $100,000.

That barely scratched the surface of what was needed. As a result, the highway's organizers — led by Indy 500 founder and Miami Beach developer Carl Foster — could only scrape together enough money to show what the finished product would look like. Short paved sections known as "seedling miles" were scattered along its length in places like Lake County, Indiana, and Grand Island, Nebraska.

Out west, the road was little more than a rutted cart path connecting far-flung towns, and nowhere more so than along the future U.S. 50 in Nevada.

If you think it's desolate now, you should have seen it then.

The *Complete Official Guide to the Lincoln Highway*, published in 1915, put it bluntly: "Wyoming, Utah and Nevada have no hard-surfaced roads, nor can they be expected there where the long mileage through a sparsely populated country would make the cost prohibitive. But the spirit is there and all that can be done to aid the tourist is done by the individual ranchers along the route, as well as by state and county officials."

Four years later, things hadn't gotten much better. Future President Dwight Eisenhower, then a lieutenant colonel in the Army, accompanied a military caravan across the country on the Lincoln Highway to see how easy it was to traverse the continent in wartime, if need be.

It turned out not to be easy at all — particularly through the rugged Western states.

"From Orr's Ranch, Utah, to Carson City, Nevada, the road is one succession of dust, ruts, pits, and holes," Eisenhower wrote. "This stretch was not improved in any way, and consisted only of a track across the desert. At many points on the road, water is 20 miles distant, and parts of the road are 90 miles from the nearest railroad."

Eisenhower and the Army convoy traveled the road from east to west. For the most part, that's the direction people traveled, so that's the direction this book will take in its tour across Nevada. Our journey starts in Ely and makes its way across to the edge of California, where the desert scrub at last gives way to the Sierra oasis that is Lake Tahoe.

U.S. 50's course doesn't follow the Lincoln Highway trajectory perfectly, deviating from it in a number of places. And even the Lincoln road itself changed course on occasion, though for the most part it followed the old Pony Express route

One old alignment of the Lincoln Highway runs north of U.S. 50 near Hickison Summit, once used by motorists climbing up from a long, straight stretch of road that heads west out of Eureka. This climb was so steep it was known as Ford's Defeat, because it proved more than a match for early Model T's.

Another stretch of the old road passes through a canyon east of Austin rather than winding its way up over the mountains, as it does now. The old route is a dirt road that enters town from the east near a white water tank.

West of Austin, the highway originally went through New Pass, but in 1924 shifted to follow what's now State Route 722 or Carroll Summit Road. This route across Carroll Summit and Railroad Pass was 15 miles shorter and more scenic. It remained part of the highway for more than four decades, until a new highway was built over New Pass and Cold Springs in 1967.

The Lincoln Highway diverges from U.S. 50 just west of Carroll Summit

Road to run directly past Middlegate Station, which is set a little way back from the current highway to the south.

Near Fernley, the highway once followed Farm District Road along State Route 828, a nearly eight-mile stretch that parallels the current U.S. 50 Alternate between Fernley and Hazen.

Left to follow rutted, often washed-out dirt roads across salt flats and through mountain passes, it was easy for travelers to lose their bearings — especially when highways weren't the uninterrupted stretches of road they are today. Instead, they were cobbled together from existing city streets (mostly unpaved), country lanes and dirt roads.

The 1923 *Automobile Blue Book* described how to get to Ely from the Utah-Nevada state line as a series of forks, twists, and turns:

You'd continue on the same road for about 23 miles in Nevada, passing Tippett's Ranch — a working ranch that's still there today. Then you'd take the left fork and cross a divide 10 miles later, bearing right at another fork and descending a downgrade. The road ended five miles after that at Stone Cabin Ranch, so you'd turn right and pass Anderson Ranch as you ascended the grade and went through Schellbourne Pass.

By this time, you'd have been in Nevada for about 47 miles, but your odyssey to Ely was far from complete. Three miles west on the other side of Schellbourne Pass, you'd turn left at Burke's Ranch, then continue past Magnuson Ranch about 11 miles farther on. You'd stay on this road for about 29 miles before taking the left fork and then bearing immediately to your right through the town of McGill.

Less than half a mile later, you'd take the right fork at the baseball grounds, onto a gravel highway before arriving in East Ely at Avenue C and 11th Street. Four more turns — left on 11th, then an immediate right, another left a mile later, and a final right at the power plant — would deposit you in Ely itself on Aultman Street. That was (and still is) the Lincoln Highway through town.

A sign east of Grantsville, Utah, shows the distances to that town, Ely, and San Francisco. *Effie Price Gladding, Across the Continent by the Lincoln Highway, 1915*

Got all that?

Good, because that's just a sample of the kind of navigating you had to do across the Lincoln Highway back in the early days. There weren't any convenience stores back then, so scattered ranches served as waystations, and motorists relied on friendly landowners and ranch hands to provide directions, a bite to eat, or water for their radiator.

There were a few (relatively) long distances spent on the same road: a 33-mile stretch outside Ely on the way to Eureka, two stretches of nearly 20 miles heading to Austin, and a couple of more between there and Fallon. But forks in the road were numerous, and you had to know where to turn, or you'd be lost in a heartbeat.

In the beginning, motorists relied on Lincoln Highway markers painted in red, white, and blue on telephone poles and fenceposts to ensure they were on the right track. But eventually, things got a little easier: In 1928, the Boy Scouts undertook a project to place some 3,000 concrete pillars along the Lincoln Highway (various accounts range from 2,600 to 4,000, the Boy Scouts' figure), each with a distinctive "L," a Lincoln medallion, and an arrow to serve as a directional marker.

You can still see many such markers along the road today, nearly a century later, but the majority are replicas. As time went on, hundreds of the original markers were moved to make way for road-widening projects, while others were stolen by opportunists who wanted a keepsake.

On the highway, 1916

> "The Lincoln Highway between Reno and Ely, Nevada, extends through five counties, Washoe, Churchill, Lander, Eureka, and White Pine, a distance of 336 miles, the greater part of which is over unsettled and desert country. Many sections are used but little for local traffic, the main travel being trans-continental, and on account of little local traffic they have been neglected in some places."
>
> **W.H. Lynch and H.E. Stewart**
> ***Report of Inspection of the Lincoln Highway***
> ***from Reno to Ely, Nevada***

U.S. 50 in Nevada is so empty and isolated in places that it's even attracted reports of ghosts, such as a lonely man hitchhiking between Ely and Ruth.

At times, you can look for miles down a straight expanse of road and not see a single car.

So how did U.S. 50 become the America's loneliest highway?

There are two big reasons it seems so isolated. First of all, many of the towns along its path are mining towns that boomed between the 1860s and the first decade of the 20th century. By the time the Lincoln Highway came along, the booms had gone bust, the miners had moved on, and the towns were in decline.

Places like Hamilton, Lane City, Austin, and Eureka saw their heyday in the 19th century. Only a few places along the highway, such as Ely, Fallon, and Carson City, survived and prospered in the 20th.

As the decades passed, many of the stops along U.S. 50 became near-ghost towns, while others such as Kimberley and Riepetown disappeared entirely. And there just isn't much traffic between ghost towns.

Second, and just as important, the Lincoln Highway lost its battle to become the primary east-west route through Nevada. Yes, U.S. 50 largely followed its path across the state. But there's no interstate there: Instead, Nevada's east-west interstate, I-80, follows the course of the old Victory Highway through Elko and Winnemucca to the north before dipping down into Reno.

What did the Victory Highway have that the Lincoln didn't? Two things: a more direct route through Utah and money from San Francisco. Lincoln Highway backers recognized their winding, poorly maintained road through Utah was a hardship on travelers. So Goodyear president Frank Seiberling gave Utah $100,000 to build a straighter, improved road along the Lincoln route.

But San Francisco interests didn't like the idea, fearing drivers would be tempted to divert from the Lincoln down to Los Angeles via the Midland Trail. Instead, they touted a direct route from Salt Lake City west across the salt flats to Wendover instead, and the California State Automobile Association (based in San Francisco, of course) came out with a study recommending the route over the Lincoln alternative.

When Utah declined to spend any more money on the Goodyear Cutoff — just $10 in 1920 — Lincoln Highway backers had little choice but to reroute their own road along the Victory Highway between Salt Lake and West Wendover, at which point they directed traffic south to Ely along a route that would become U.S. 93. Construction of that route between Wendover and McGill, however, was not approved and surveyed until 1928. It was part of U.S. 50 until 1953, when it was moved south and cosigned with U.S. 6 east of Ely. In fact, it continued to be identified on maps as 50 Alternate all the way up until 1977.

Even when the 50/93 route was in place, however, it was a significant detour, and many drivers found it easier and more direct to simply follow the Victory Highway on west from Wendover through Elko and Winnemucca. The federal government apparently agreed with their assessment, earmarking 60 percent of Nevada's public highway money to the Victory Highway: just over $2 million.

The Lincoln Highway Association appealed that decision — and lost.

As a result, the Victory Highway became the preferred traffic corridor through Nevada, and the Lincoln became America's Loneliest Road.

How to use this book

For most of its journey through Nevada, U.S. Highway 50 roughly follows the course laid out by the Lincoln Highway. But in some places, the Lincoln's path has been taken up by other federal roads: U.S. 93 Alternate and 93 north of Ely; U.S. 395 from Reno down through Carson City; U.S. 50 Alternate from Fallon northwest to Fernley; and U.S. 40 from Fernley west through Crystal Bay on the north shore of Lake Tahoe.

In one section, going southeast out of Ely, U.S. 50 follows its own path, entirely separate from the Lincoln Highway, which originally followed Nevada State Routes 2 and 893 across the Schell Creek Range from Utah.

As mentioned earlier, this book moves east to west along the Lincoln Highway. Highway shields for the various roads will appear whenever the old highway's course moves from one modern highway to another. So, if you see a shield for U.S. 50, everything from that point on will appear on that route until a different shield appears.

The Lincoln Highway marker indicates the section covering State Routes 2 and 893 mentioned earlier.

Also included are a few significant detours to interesting places off the main route: Cherry Creek, Great Basin National Park, Ione, Berlin, Fort Churchill, Silver City, Gold Hill, and Virginia City.

Short features show what it was like to travel on the early Lincoln Highway in the form of guidebook directions and travelers' accounts.

If you want to follow the road from west to east, simply start at the back and make your way toward the front.

This book serves as a great companion to the "Nevada Highway 50 Survival Challenge" passport program. The program issues "survival guides" with maps that serve as "passports," which participants can get stamped by participating businesses and civic organizations along the way.

Once your passport has been stamped at five of the eight communities from Baker to Carson City, you keep it as a souvenir and tear off the back flap, which you can mail in to receive a Highway 50 Survivor certificate. For details on this program, stop by participating chambers of commerce, vendors, and museums, or see the following websites:

- https://loneliestroad.us/highway-50-survival-guide/
- https://issuu.com/travelnevada/docs/hwy50survivalguide

To follow the Lincoln Highway through Nevada, check out the online virtual interactive map on the Lincoln Highway Association's website at https://www.lincolnhighwayassoc.org/map/.

Itinerary

Stop	Page
West Wendover	22
Tippett's Ranch	27
Schellbourne Pass	30
Detour – Cherry Creek	34
McGill	37
Ely	42
Detour – Great Basin National Park	53
Lane City	64
Riepetown	70
Kimberley	71
Ruth	72

Continued on next page

Stop	Page
Hamilton	74
Eureka	83
Austin	104
Carroll Summit	129
Eastgate	132
Middlegate	135
Detour – Ione	137
Detour – Berlin	138
Westgate	139
Frenchman's Station	140
Stillwater	147
Fallon	149
Hazen	166
Fernley	170
Wadsworth	175
Sparks	179
Reno	192
Verdi	203
Crystal Bay	204
Washoe Valley	206
Silver Springs	217
Detour – Fort Churchill	218
Stagecoach	220
Sutro	221
Dayton	224
Detour – Silver City	232
Detour – Gold Hill	234
Detour – Virginia City	237
Mound House	246
Carson City	253
Glenbrook	269
Cave Rock	270
Zephyr Cove	271
Stateline	274

Main Street, McGill. *Author photo*

A dinosaur keeps watch over U.S. 93 outside the Prospector Hotel and Casino in Ely. *Author photo*

The loneliest Road in America

Utah State Line to Ely

If you're coming into Northern Nevada today from the east, you have a couple of choices: You can head through West Wendover on Interstate 80 and keep going west from there through Elko to Reno, or you can enter the state more than 150 miles to the south by taking U.S. Highway 50 past the Great Basin National Park and on into Ely.

The original alignment of the Lincoln Highway didn't follow either of those routes. Rather, it crossed the mountains as a narrow, winding road from Ibapah, Utah, past isolated stops such as Tippett's Ranch and Schellbourne Ranch (both of which are still operating) before depositing travelers at an old Pony Express stop on a road that's now U.S. Highway 93. There's a rest stop there these days, across from an abandoned store and motel.

A later alignment of the Lincoln Highway went through West Wendover and down U.S. 93 Alternate to 93, then joined the earlier route at the Pony Express stop. Here in Eastern Nevada, on into Ely, is one of the few places U.S. 50 doesn't follow the old Lincoln. The two join up in central Ely at the modern junction of 50 and 93, which is just west of the historic train depot that now doubles as a museum.

Before they do, though, the Lincoln Highway travels through McGill, a historic town with a 1905 pharmacy that's on the National Register of Historic Places and has been converted into a museum.

Top: A car stops at the Utah-Nevada state line on the Lincoln Highway in 1918. *University of Michigan Special Collections Research Center*

Above: Marker at the state line in 1940. *Arthur Rothstein, Library of Congress*

On the highway, 1915

"In the past, motorists have shown some hesitancy about making the trip from Salt Lake City to Ely, Nevada, crossing a small part of the desert, because of the promiscuous circulation of advice as to extra equipment which should be carried. It is advisable to take a thermos bottle of iced water, or a desert water bag and some food in case one is held up with tire or engine trouble, but other than that, no extras are needed."

The Complete Official Road Guide to the Lincoln Highway

On the highway, 1918

"Gravel to McGill; balance natural prairie and desert road. Just beyond Kearney's Ranch the route crosses a section of the Great American desert and will be found almost impassable after a heavy rain."

Automobile Blue Book, Vol. 8

Getting There

Some directions in the 1913 Lincoln Highway Directory, with miles between each entry:

Tippett's: Keep straight ahead; fork to left. Keep straight ahead.

3.6 miles: Spring to left.

0.3 miles: Dim road comes in from left.

6.7 miles: Forks; take new road to right, going up.

1.0 mile: Top of divide.

0.2 mile: Forks; keep to left.

0.5 mile: Forks; keep to right.

0.3 mile: Jeff Davis peak, highest peak in Nevada, way off to left. Altitude, 13,200 feet.

1.8 miles: Main forks. Turn right, going north up valley.

1.3 miles: Forks; keep to right, going north; sign posts here.

West Wendover

The Stateline Service Hotel, top, in the 1940s and Nevada Club in the 1930s, both in West Wendover. Bill Smith and partner Herman Eckstein founded the Stateline as a service station and garage called the Cobble Stone along the highway in 1926, then expanded it to include a 15-room hotel with a casino when gambling was legalized in 1931. Smith, by then sole owner, opened a new air-conditioned hotel in 1935. The casino became the Wendover Nugget in 2004. *Special Collections and University Archives Department, University of Nevada, Reno*

This garage in Wendover, Utah, just across the state line from West Wendover, bore the name of the Victory Highway. But the Lincoln Highway shared the so-called Wendover Route, as well — although not by choice. The Lincoln Highway had originally been designed to run to the south through Utah, along a planned "Goodyear Cutoff" that crossed the state line just west of Ibapah. The Lincoln Highway Association gave the state of Utah a significant sum of money to improve the route. But interests in San Francisco countered with money of their own to invest in the Wendover Route over the Salt Flats. When Utah never used the Goodyear funds but worked to build the Wendover Route instead, the LHA ultimately acquiesced and rerouted the Lincoln Highway through Wendover. *University of Michigan Special Collections Research Center*

Finding West Wendover
Location: Just west of Utah-Nevada state line on U.S. 93 Alternate, 108 miles south of West Wendover

Route: Opal Drive (Lincoln Highway), Wendover Boulevard (U.S. 93)

"Wendover Will" points the way to the Stateline Casino in West Wendover sometime after the giant cowboy was installed in 1952. *Special Collections and University Archives Department, University of Nevada, Reno*

An old three-mile segment of the Lincoln Highway leaves West Wendover and continues south from I-80 along U.S. 93 Alternate toward U.S. 93 and Ely. There, 93 hooks up with U.S. 50, which heads west and branches off Southeast to Baker. *Historic American Engineering Record, Library of Congress*

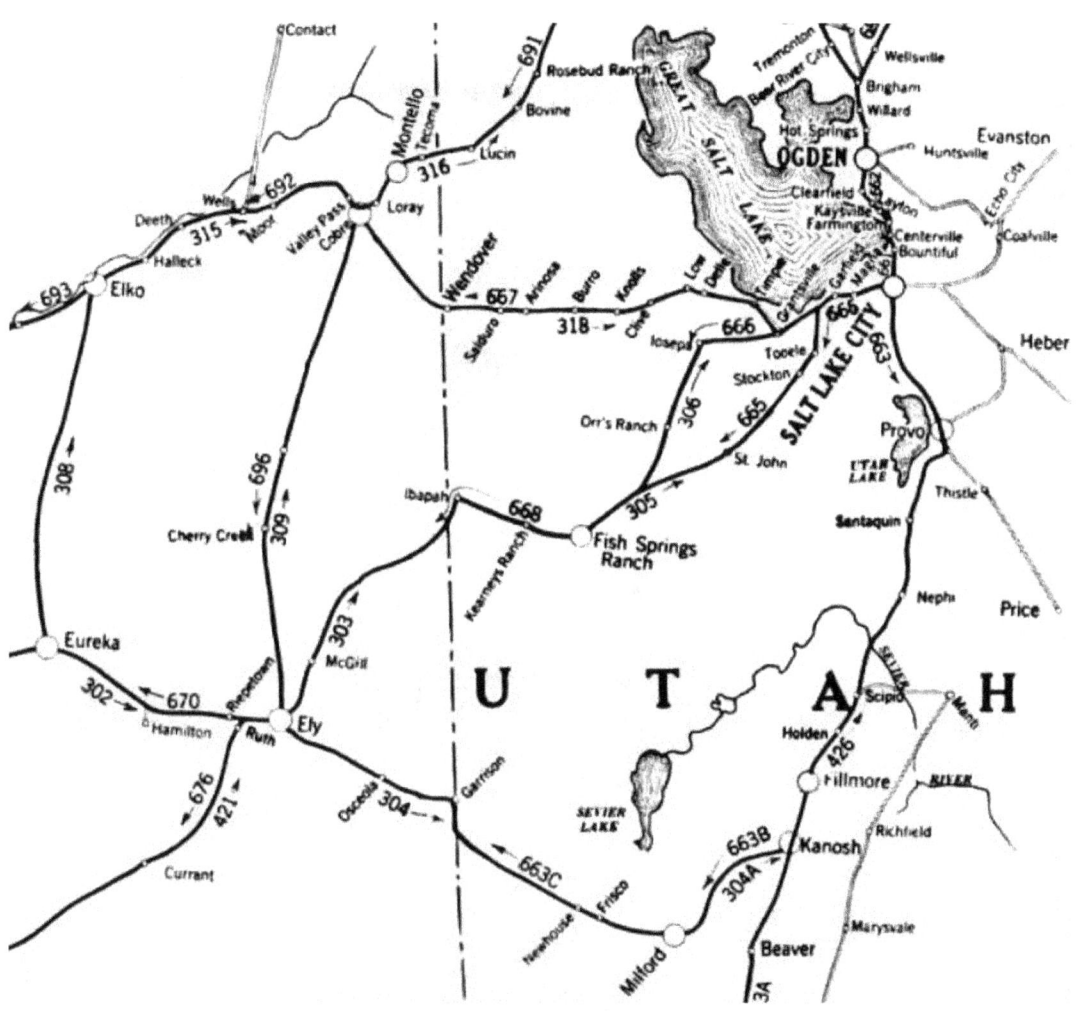

This map from a 1918 travel guide shows the road east over the Salt Flats through Wendover and the road that headed southwest from Salt Lake City before crossing the state line to the south, near Ibapah.

A billboard invites motorists to choose between U.S. 50 and U.S. 40.
Nevada Department of Transportation

Tippett's Ranch

Above: A sign east of Tippett's Ranch touts the Lincoln Highway via Reno and Sacramento as the "most direct route" to California's scenic wonders, declaring the road to be "well marked by the California Automobile Association" in this undated photo. *University of Michigan Special Collections Research Center*

Left: 1917 letter between Tippett Mercantile and Becker Brewing. *Lincoln Highway Collection of Russell Rein*

Ruins at Tippett's Ranch along the first alignment of the Lincoln Highway. The 1916 Lincoln Highway Guide said it had a camp site and general store in sight of "snowcapped Mt. Wheeler" to the south. *Author photos*

An early photo of Tippett's Ranch. *University of Michigan Special Collections Research Center*

On the highway, 1915

"...we crossed Shellbourne Pass (sic) under the shadow of the Shellbourne range. We passed some young people from Detroit, the gentleman driving his car. We also passed some men with their laden burros taking supplies to the sheepmen in the mountain ranges. These sheepmen live their lives apart from the world for months at a time, seeing only the man who brings their supplies at intervals.

"We had luncheon at Anderson's ranch, where they treated us very hospitably. I judged that this was a Mormon's household, as Mormon marriage certificates hung upon the wall and as the Deseret Weekly was evidently it's newspaper connection to the outside world. ..."

"...we passed Tippett's ranch (sic) and learned that its owner travels thirty-six miles for his mail and supplies."

Effie Price Gladding,
Across the Continent by the Lincoln Highway

Schellbourne Pass

Top: Stone house on Lincoln Highway east of Schellbourne Pass.

Above: Sign near Schellbourne Ranch: "This route follows the first transcontinental telegraph line used from 1861 to 1869. Completion of this line led to the end of the Pony Express Mail Service. Stumps of telegraph poles remain along the route." *Author photos*

AMERICA'S LONELIEST ROAD

According to the 1916 Lincoln Highway Guide, Schellbourne was a "ranch and post office, once a government post on the emigrant trail and pony express." Amenities included "meals, lodging, drinking water, radiator water, [and a] camp site." *Author photos*

This abandoned gas stop, bar, and motel decays across from an old Pony Express station, now a rest stop, where the old Lincoln Highway meets U.S. 93. *Author photos*

On the highway, 1923

"Natural prairie road to McGill; balance gravel highway. Except for some rough stretches near Ibapah [Utah], average conditions on this trip are fair and good time can be made when weather conditions are favorable. The route traverses sparsely settled hilly sagebrush country. Meals and supplies may be had at frequent intervals at various ranches..."

Automobile Blue Book, Vol. 4

Heading east on the original Lincoln Highway after crossing Schellbourne Pass. *Author photo*

Detour: Cherry Creek

An eight-mile detour off U.S. 93 Alternate on State Route 489, just north of the old Lincoln Highway junction and old Pony Express stop. You won't see any of these historic buildings there today, though; they burned in a 1972 fire. *White Pine Historical Society Photo Collection, East Ely Depot Museum*

The Cherry Creek Saloon, once one of 27 in town, opened in 1883 and was the last one standing. *Author photo*

The Cherry Creek Schoolhouse, built in 1872, had a real blackboard and was divided down the middle, with a curtain separating the lower- and upper-grade students. A new schoolhouse was built in 1940. The original one, with its bell at top right, is now the town museum. *Author photos*

An old building and abandoned gas pump in Cherry Creek, 2022. At its height, 6,000 people lived in Cherry Creek; the 2010 census counted just 72. *Author photos*

U.S. 93 through McGill, lined with buildings including the McGill Club, third from left, a former movie house, one door farther down, and a café. *Author photo*

McGill

County: White Pine
Elevation: 6,204
Established: 1872
Unincorporated

1916

Population : 2,500

Accommodations: No hotels; several lodges and boarding houses

Features: Bank, public school, 25 general businesses, smelting plant

2022

Population: 1,148 (2010)

On the highway, 1921

"McGill, paralleling Garfield [Utah], lies across the valley [from Ely] on a hill, a grey-white block of mill buildings and concentration plants. It was still and silent! The compact mass of tin roofs blinked idly in the sun."

William Ellwell Onions

McGill was originally known as "Smelter," because there was a smelter there — and a major one. In 1916, the smelting plant was handling 12,000 to 15,000 tons of copper ore a day. The town ultimately took its name from McGill Ranch, which had been established back in 1872 and had a post office that opened there in 1891.

The Steptoe Valley Smelting and Mining Company, later Nevada Consolidated, was the big business in town. Nevada Consolidated brought in copper ore from Ruth, just west of Ely, for processing.

McGill's population reached its peak in 1930 at just over 3,000, and two years later, Nevada Consolidated was acquired by Kennecott Utah Copper. But the number of residents declined as the region's copper reserves were gradually depleted and production costs rose after the 1950s.

Ultimately, Kennecott shut down the smelter in 1983 and had it demolished, depriving McGill of its primary source of economic stability.

Finding McGill

Location: 108 miles south of West Wendover
              12 miles north of Ely
Route: Great Basin Highway (Lincoln Highway, U.S. 93)

McGill as it appeared in the spring of 1964. *Courtesy McGill Drug Store Museum*

Steptoe Valley Smelting built the McGill Clubhouse in 1911 to house unmarried employees in 36 dormitories and provide its workers with recreational activities. The building featured a gym, library, basketball court, pool tables, and two-lane bowling alley (which was converted into a shooting gallery in the 1940s). Civic and social events were held there until 1959.

The McGill Drug Store has been preserved as a museum in the condition it was in when it closed in 1983. Out front are original and replica Lincoln Highway markers. *Author photos*

McGill in 1940. *Arthur Rothstein, Library of Congress*

Frosty Stand is closed along the highway through McGill. The Drakulich brothers opened the business on March 1, 1957, as Bob's Drive In. *Author photo*

Looking down Aultman Avenue, with the Hotel Nevada at right, in the 1940s. *Special Collections and University Archives Department, University of Nevada, Reno*

Ely

County: White Pine *(county seat since 1887)*
Elevation: 6,347
Established: 1868

1916

    Population : 3,500

    Accommodations: 6 hotels

    Features: 1 garage, 3 banks, 3 newspapers, 100 general businesses

2022

    Population : 3,924 (2020)

The Hotel Nevada on U.S. 50.
Author photo

First thing to remember: It's pronounced E-lee, not E-lie.

The 1916 Lincoln Highway Association road guide noted that the speed limit through town was 12 miles per hour, but it wasn't enforced. It was getting easier to speed, too, since there was "extensive road improvement" in town.

Originally a stop on the Pony Express route, the town got kickstarted in 1906 with the discovery of copper, subsequently eclipsing nearby boomtowns like Hamilton and Lane City. Unlike those now-ghost towns, it survived and remains the largest city in White Pine County. It's also the county seat, having assumed that distinction in 1887, when it replaced Hamilton.

The Northern Hotel was a major stop along the Lincoln Highway, offering rooms with a bath for $2 and rooms without one for half that price.

Built by Goldfield residents Tex Rickard, the famous boxing promoter, and Ole Elliott in 1906, the three-story Northern was destroyed by fire in 1964. The $400,000 Hotel Nevada, which is still in business, opened its doors in 1929. At six stories, it was the tallest building in the state at the time, and held that distinction for the next two years.

Finding Ely

Location: 12 miles south of McGill

3 miles east of Lane City

Route: U.S. 93, U.S. 50

- *First Lincoln Highway:* Avenue C to 11th Street to Aultman Avenue
- *Second Lincoln Highway:* Avenue C to Aultman at Nevada Avenue

The Ely Mercantile was selling hats, caps, shoes, dry goods, groceries, notions, and general merchandise in 1906 when this photo was taken. *Public domain*

Looking north along the original Lincoln Highway toward U.S. 93 in the distance at the east end of Ely. *Author photo*

Lincoln Highway Garage Company
ELY, NEVADA

Official register and road logs in all directions free. A full line of automobile supplies, tires and accessories. Special attention given to Transcontinental Tourists. A complete first class repair shop in connection. Satisfied customers our method of advertising.

Agents for Ford, Reo and Franklin Cars

The Lincoln Highway Garage was a recommended stop with an easy-to-remember name in Ely. The garage produced its own *Mountains to Coast Road Map* in 1918. *White Pine Historical Society Photo Collection, East Ely Depot Museum*

Ely motels from top: Town & Country on U.S. 50 just south of the 395 junction; a combination motel-liquor store at the junction; sign for the 1955 Deser-Est Motel facing a curve in Aultman Street east of downtown. *Author photos*

Top: White Pine County Middle School, originally Ely's high school, opened in 1913.

Above: The White Pine County Courthouse, built in 1908. The two historical buildings sit on opposite sides of U.S. 50 in Ely. *Author photos*

In the 1950s, Ely's Bank Club boasted "We Never Close," but at some point, it did close. It's now known as Mr. G's, which once had a brothel on the second floor and was connected to the Hotel Nevada across the street via (now sealed and supposedly haunted) underground tunnels. Next door, the Ely Theatre opened in 1916 as the Capitol and lasted until 1964. *Special Collections and University Archives Department, University of Nevada, Reno*

The same section of Aultman looking the opposite direction today. *Author photo*

Top: A historic photo shows the entrance to the Hotel Nevada. *The Lincoln Highway Collection of Russell Rein*

Above: Stars on a "walk of fame" honor famous people who've stayed at the hotel, including Ely native first lady Pat Nixon and author Stephen King. Rooms inside are dedicated to other famous guests, including Mickey Rooney and Charley Pride. "Nevada's first fireproof hotel" was built to capitalize on traffic coming down the new segment of road from West Wendover.

Right: A prospector stands over the entry to the hotel's Nevada Club. *Author photos*

If you enter Ely from the west, you'll find this old Richfield station (below) on one side, and the Big 4 Ranch (above) on the other. The Big 4, founded in 1880, advertises itself as the oldest brothel in Nevada. It also offers a saloon, massage parlor, and regular motel rooms. It's also said to be haunted by the ghost of an angry woman whose wayward husband passed away there.
Author photos

On the highway, 1921

"There is a really very good Main street in Ely. A number of large stores, cafes, candy shops and garages compose this thoroughfare. The garages and vulcanizing shops entirely outnumber the other places of business, by proportion, and immediately suggest an amendment to Sinclair Lewis's description of Gopher Prairie...

"One street, about a block in length, was completely lined on both sides by 'cribs,' the common name for the hovel which the common woman [sic] of the mining camps inhabit. Each crib was stuck to the side of the other, so that they formed a continuous line of small, wooden, box-like rooms, each with a door and a window opening on the street. The line on one side of the street was unbroken except for an establishment that had the air of a saloon, with its wide doors and brass fixings here and there.

"The saloon place was O'Niels Place, and its wide mouth was egress to twenty five or thirty other cribs situated, or rather, hidden in its rear. There must have been about one hundred and fifty of these places. As I walked up the wooden side walk, wondering about the feet and the folly and the tragedy that had passed over these same boards, I saw that each little window had a card hung in it. These cards had the names of the occupants on them: Mary, Rose, Helen, Doll, were some of the names I remember. Over each door was an electric meter, and somehow that spinning disc measured more than kilowatts — it measured life for each one of those strange, fallen creatures who lived in her wooden box like cell."

William Ellwell Onions

The Nevada Northern Railway depot in East Ely was built in 1907 not far from where the Lincoln Highway would pass through town. The railroad was originally owned by the Nevada Consolidated Copper Company; passenger service ended in 1941, and the depot is now a national historic register site that houses a museum. *Author photos*

Detour: Great Basin National Park

One place where U.S. 50 diverges from the Lincoln Highway is in Ely, where it travels southeast to the Utah state line. Just before you get there, you'll hit the Great Basin National Park, which offers sights like Lehman Cave, left, and Wheeler Peak, Nevada's second-tallest mountain, below. *Author photos*

Absalom Lehman discovered this series of caverns and began offering guided tours in the 1880s. According to legend, he was riding his horse when it broke through a thin layer covering the natural entrance above the cave. Bats live in the cave, and 10 species can be found in the area. *Author photo*

The Great Basin bristlecone pine grows in Nevada, Utah, and eastern California. Bristlecones can live up to 4,800 years, making them one of the most enduring species on Earth. *Author photos*

U.S. 50 through Eureka. *Author photo*

U.S. 50 west of Ely.
Author photo

The loneliest Road in America

Ely to Eureka

When you get on the road west of Ely, heading toward Eureka, you understand why U.S. 50 became graced with the nickname "The Loneliest Road in America." There's not much between Ely and Eureka.

There's Ruth, just outside town and a little more than a mile to the south, a small mining community where a few people still live.

Other than that, most of what you'll encounter is a mixture of sagebrush, dirt devils, and, if you're lucky, a few pronghorns: desert-dwellers that look like either antelopes or goats, but which are actually more closely related to the giraffe. Good luck trying to get a picture of them, though. They're the fastest animals in North America, bounding in and out of view at a moment's notice.

The original Lincoln Highway swung south past Ruth, away from the current U.S. 50, for 10 miles or so in what's actually a more direct route, rejoining the modern highway briefly at Moorman Ranch (which still exists and boasts an original Lincoln Highway marker). It then made another detour south toward Hamilton, the original seat of White Pine County.

By the time the highway was built, though, Hamilton's mining boom had gone bust, and the town was very much in decline. So the highway builders

Getting There

Directions for navigating the first Lincoln Highway from the 1913 directory, with miles between each entry, beginning at White Pine Summit, almost 40 miles west of Ely:

0.1 mile: Take right fork signboard (left to Hamilton 5 miles).

2.0 miles: Take left fork.

2.0 miles: Six-mile house.

0.1 mile: Curve around barn to right and keep right.

0.5 mile: Left fork, signboard (right to Newark).

1.1 miles: Right fork.

7.8 miles: Left fork.

1.0 mile: Pancake Summit.

7.2 miles: 14-Mile House, signboard, water (not fit to drink). Curve left around corral and go south.

2.6 miles: Old telephone line comes in here, which continues to Eureka.

also set up a short bypass that allowed motorists to avoid a sharp V-shaped trip down into Hamilton and back north again.

It wasn't long before the Lincoln Highway builders abandoned that route entirely and built a new road where U.S. 50 is today. Both roads came back together around 14 Mile House, and the highway then followed the path of today's Highway 50 up to Pinto Summit at 7,376 feet.

As you travel U.S. 50, it can seem like series of roller-coaster rides interspersed with long sections of straightaway.

The modern highway travels through 17 mountain passes in Nevada, all but five of them at least 6,000 feet high (and another, Devils Gate west of Eureka, nearly that high at 5,990 feet).

The 1913 Lincoln Highway Guide mentions places that are nearly impossible to identify such as Riepetown and Kimberley. But there are also ghost towns, like Hamilton and Lane City, that still exist in the form of a few tumble-down buildings.

There wasn't much at 14 Mile House when this photo was taken in 1920, and according to the Lincoln Highway Directory, the water wasn't fit to drink.
University of Michigan Special Collections Research Center

The dirt road to Hamilton is both deserted and treacherous, strewn with rocks and gullies. Four-wheel drive is recommended, and try not to get stranded there: Cellular signals are spotty at best, and you aren't likely to see another motorist. No one goes to Hamilton anymore. *Author photo*

Clouds loom over a section of the old highway near Hamilton. *Author photo*

On the highway, 1915

"We saw hundreds of prairie dogs. Day after day, they scuttled across our pathway, often narrowly escaping… We sometimes saw a coyote, usually in the early morning or late afternoon… And once we saw a beautiful antelope leaping and bounding over the sage brush so lightly that he looked in the distance like a phantom animal of thistle down."

Effie Price Gladding,
Across the Continent by the Lincoln Highway

On the highway, 1918

"Dirt and gravel road with several rough and sandy stretches. Use caution to keep supplies replenished."

Automobile Blue Book, Vol. 8

On the highway, 1921

"We passed Riepetown and then Kimberly. Riepetown, Bob told me is known as 'The Town that God Forgot,' and [h]as the wickedest collection of tumble down abodes in Nevada. Kimberly has been a great copper and silver mining camp. Now it is dead and empty."

William Ellwell Onions

A water tank between Ely and Eureka describes the desolate nature of this section of road. *Author photo*

On the highway, 1923

"First 36 miles gravel highway; balance unimproved prairie road. Huge, treeless flats, separated by shrub covered mountain ranges are intermittently traversed on this trip. The country is uninteresting, and with the exception of a few ranches and a small mining town no habitation is encountered. Meals and supplies may be had at Hamilton, a small mining settlement one-half mile from the highway."

Automobile Blue Book, Vol. 4

Lane City

County: White Pine
Elevation: 6,598
Established: 1869 as Mineral City
Ghost town

1916
    Population: 100
    Accommodations: Camp site
    Features: Drinking water, radiator water, telephone, telegraph

2022
    Population: 0
    Features: Abandoned schoolhouse, ruined homes

As you head out of Ely, you'll pass a railroad tunnel, then round a curve. Just down the road from there, you may notice a large white building that looks like a church. Actually, it's a schoolhouse, boarded up and lonesome surrounded by sagebrush.

If you pull off the road there, you'll see an old section of the Lincoln Highway, but if you look more closely, you'll find something else, as well. On closer inspection, you'll find the schoolhouse is just one of several buildings within walking distance along the highway, all of them stone or wooden dwellings in various states of extreme disrepair.

Welcome to Lane City, formerly known as Mineral City, a mining town that boasted as many as 600 residents around 1872. It was the area's first major settlement, with an economy powered by silver deposits found in the area in 1867. A small smelter and a 10-stamp mill were constructed.

In addition to the schoolhouse and miners' homes, the town once boasted six saloons, four boarding houses, and a few shops. It even had a post office. There's no sign of those now, but several ruins remain in the foothills beside the road.

Mineral City tapped out in 1880, but an eastern investor named Charles Lane restarted up the stamp mill in 1896, and the town enjoyed a brief revival under his name. The post office reopened in 1902.

But the "new era" was over by 1910, when the mines were abandoned, and the post office closed again the following year. A few miners continued to live there for years, though, into the 1950s, traveling to work in Ely or Ruth. The ruins of their dwellings are the ones that remain today.

Finding Lane City

Location: 3 miles west of Ely

Route: Short section of Lincoln Highway running parallel, north of U.S. 50

The schoolhouse at Lane City is the only non-residential structure remaining in the ghost town.
Author photo

Abandoned residences at Lane City. *Author photos*

The Lincoln Highway in Lane City and some rusted metal left behind by a wrecked car. *Author photos*

Top: The Red Rooster Bar was the last business open in Lane City. The building, now gone, carried an ad for Becker's Beer. *Nevada Historical Society*

Above: An overview of Lane City before it was a ghost town. *White Pine Historical Society Photo Collection, East Ely Depot Museum*

Lane City ruins alongside the Lincoln Highway. *Author photos*

Riepetown

Riepetown was on the Lincoln Highway in 1913 and listed in the *1916 Complete Official Road Guide* (where it was called "Reipetown") as having a railroad station, gas, drinking water, radiator water, and telephone service. You could also get plenty of booze. Riepetown was known as "the wettest town in the county" in 1909, a thriving center for both liquor and prostitution. Customers came from nearby Ruth and Kimberly, just a mile up the road, to patronize its 16 saloons and "cribs," or shacks for prostitution. If you were in Riepetown on the Lincoln Highway, you were 2,735 miles from New York City and 596 miles from San Francisco. A fire destroyed the town in 1917, and it was rebuilt, but nothing remains of it today.
Public domain

Kimberley

Kimberley, whose post office opened in 1905 and remained open until 1958, had a newspaper (the *Kimberley News*), school, hospital, and a population listed at 300 in the 1916 *Complete Official Road Guide*. A company town, it was named for Peter Kimberley, an investor in the Giroux Mining Company that started to develop the site to mine for copper there in 1900. Consolidated Copper bought out Giroux in 1914, and the town grew to nearly 460 residents by 1920. The Complete and Official Guide to the Lincoln Highway in 1916 called it "an interesting point to tarry," with meals, lodging, drinking water, and radiator water to be had there. More than 1,000 residents lived there a decade later, but Kennecott Copper bought the mine in 1958 and shut down the mills. Like Riepetown, Kimberley no longer exists today; the town was replaced by an open-pit mine. *White Pine Historical Society Photo Collection, East Ely Depot Museum*

Ruth

The Ruth Community Presbyterian Church, top, was built around 1925. The original town was surrounded by a huge open-pit copper mine. The town just south of U.S. 50 had 500 residents by 1910 and amenities including a hospital, bunkhouses, and boarding houses supplied by Nevada Consolidated Copper. Above: Mine tailings at Ruth, seen from U.S. 50. *Author photos*

Miners' homes, above, line the rim of the Ruth mine pit, seen here in 1940.
Arthur Rothstein, Library of Congress

Hamilton

County: White Pine *(county seat, 1869 to 1887)*
Elevation: 8,058
Established: 1868 as Cave City
Ghost town

1916
    Population: 67 (1920)
2022
    Population: 0
    Features: Ruins of former hotel, Wells Fargo office, other structures

Hamilton isn't much to look at these days: just ruins, along with an old cemetery. In fact, when it comes to those ruins, there are fewer than those that you'll find at Lane City.

But in its heyday around 1870, Hamilton was a lot more impressive than Lane City ever was. Built in rarified air, more than 8,000 feet above sea level, this mining town south of modern U.S. 50 drew thousands of prospectors at the end of the 1860s. By the summer of 1869, it boasted a population of some 12,000.

The town was a rollicking western town with nearly 100 saloons, 60 general stores, eight law offices, a Wells Fargo building, a skating rink, opera house, union and fraternal halls, and nearly 200 mining companies operating in the area. Of course, there was a red-light district, too.

A grand hotel, the J.B. Withington, opened its doors to travelers in 1869. Nearby, other boomtowns sprang up with names like Treasure City (with 6,000 residents of its own), Shermantown, and Eberhardt.

Lots purchased for $25 sold for $600 or even $1,200.

But the prosperity didn't last. The silver deposits upon which the town was built weren't enough to sustain it, and although it was named the county seat in 1869, it began to shrink rapidly in the early 1870s. Many of the residents were transient miners who quickly pulled up stakes and moved on to the next big boomtown.

By 1870, the population was just 3,913 — one-third of what it had been a year earlier. A fire in 1873 destroyed much of the business district, causing more than half a million dollars in damage, and the town's population shrank to just 500 residents.

A second fire, just after New Year's in 1885, gutted the courthouse, and the county seat moved to Ely two years later.

The June 1909 edition of *Mines and Minerals* described the once-thriving city thus:

"Today the impression one receives on viewing it, is that of a well-nigh deserted habitat of days long past. Many of the buildings spared by the [1885] fire are dilapidated and rapidly falling into decay, and the skeletons of numerous mills, big waste dumps, and its history, are all that is left to tell of its once flourishing condition."

A year after that account was published, the population had dipped to 107. Hamilton was still worth including on the original Lincoln Highway in 1913, if only barely. But it wasn't included in the 1916 *Complete Official Road Guide to the Lincoln Highway*, and you're unlikely to find anyone on that section of dirt-and-gravel road today.

The ruins of the J.B. Withington Hotel stood for many years before collapsing in an earthquake during the 1950s. After that, vandals made off with "souvenirs" from many of the town's buildings.

Finding Hamilton

Location: 48 miles west of Ely

45 miles west of Lane City

44 miles east of Eureka

Route: Old Lincoln Highway, a dirt road south of U.S. 50 that branches off from the modern highway as White Pine County Road 11 near Illipah Campground and rejoins it a few miles east of Eureka near the site of the old 14-Mile House.

A bell that once adorned the first fire engine ever used in San Francisco stands in the foreground of this photo, which shows what's left of Hamilton in the age of the automobile. *University of Michigan Special Collections Research Center*

Two men inspect the first fire engine used in San Francisco, which the town of Hamilton purchased in its heyday. As the town declined, so did the state of the fire engine and hose carriage, which the *Reno Evening Gazette* described in 1915 as being "in a sad state of dilapidation" and "half-buried in a snowdrift." The building in this photo is the J.B. Withington Hotel, which was used as the seat of county government after the $55,000 courthouse burned in 1885. The county seat moved to Ely in 1887. *University of Michigan Special Collections Research Center*

All that remained of the Withington Hotel in 2022. *Author photo*

Two more views of the Withington Hotel before it was lost to history and the sagebrush. Built for $85,000 in 1869, it was considered the finest building in Nevada at the time. It was also the site of a hanging in 1886: A man named Crutchley was executed in an upper room after a hole had been cut in the floor so he could be hung from a scaffold and dropped into the basement. Crutchley had been convicted in the fatal shooting of Cherry Creek resident John Herslett. *White Pine Historical Society Photo Collection, East Ely Depot Museum*

Stone buildings lie in ruins in Hamilton.
Sharon Stora

Little is left of once-bustling Hamilton. *Sharon Stora*

On the highway, 1915

"When we reached Six Mile House, having passed Fourteen Mile House [heading east], we asked the ranchman's wife to give us some luncheon. She said she could not accommodate us, having few supplies on hand. She advised us to go on to Hamilton and said she would telephone the Hamilton House that we were coming.

"In accordance with her directions, we took a turn to the right shortly after leaving Six Mile House and climbed up a narrow, rocky canyon road. Finally, within a mile or so of Hamilton, when we had one more hill to climb, we came upon a morass made by the bursting of a water pipe. We could not go around it and we dared not go through it, no friendly settler with a powerful horse being in sight.

"So we turned carefully about... We pressed on down the hill past a deserted ranch house to Moorman's Ranch, a hospitable looking house by the roadside. At Moorman's Ranch, we found an unforgettable hospitality. Our host and hostess were Missourians, and to our question as to whether they could give us any luncheon at 2 o'clock, they gave us a most satisfactory answer. Mrs. Moorman soon had a laden table ready for us, and we sat down to fried bacon, potatoes, lettuce, radishes, preserved cherries, stewed prunes, milk, tea, and pie."

Effie Price Gladding,
Across the Continent by the Lincoln Highway

Two views of the Moorman Ranch and the Lincoln Highway, with the latter showing an original LH marker.
Author photos

Eureka

County: Eureka *(county seat)*
Elevation: 6,826
Established: 1864
Unincorporated

1916

    Population : 785

    Accommodations: 2 hotels

    Features: Garage, newspaper, school, telegraph company, 30 general businesses

2022

    Population : 480 (2018)

    Features: 3 parks, second-largest fire house in the state built in 2009

Eureka means "I have found it!"

You won't find a lot of people in Eureka, Nevada (not to be confused with Eureka, California), but you will find plenty of history. The town was originally called Napias, after the Shoshone word for "silver," but it wasn't long before it adopted its current name.

That was appropriate, because Eureka's silver ore contained a high percentage of lead, which became the primary mineral produced there. In fact, the town churned out 118,000 tons of ore in 1878, making it the richest mineral producer in the state.

A population of 640 in 1870 had ballooned to about 9,000 by 1878, and the town built a number of impressive historic structures that line Main Street (aka U.S. 50) through town today. Unfortunately, they weren't always clearly visible during Eureka's boom years: 24 smelters belched so much smoke skyward that the town began to be called "The Pittsburgh of the West."

The Opera House, Jackson House Hotel, and Eureka County Courthouse are among the buildings visible in this overview of U.S. 50/Main Street through town. *Author photo*

At its peak, Eureka boasted six newspapers and more than 100 saloons, but flooding and fire took their toll on the town. Floodwaters claimed 17 lives in an 1874 disaster; more flooding followed two years later and again two years after that. Fires, meanwhile, struck in 1872, 1875, and (the worst) in 1879.

The cumulative effect was twofold. First, about half the residents had packed their bags by 1880, when the population was recorded at 4,207, and the town shrank even more as its silver mines began to struggle in the following decade: By 1890, just 1,609 people remained.

But while the people left, the buildings remained. After the fire of '79, residents built new structures of fire-resistant brick with iron doors to keep the flames out. As a result, many of the buildings erected during that era remain along Main Street and elsewhere in town. These include the Eureka Opera House, County Courthouse, and Eureka Sentinel building from 1879; and the Colonnade Hotel from 1880.

U.S. 50 through Eureka as it appeared in the 1930s. The Opera House, which opened in 1880, is seen in its incarnation as the Eureka Theatre movie house. It began showing silent movies in 1915 and took on its new name in the 1920s, operating as a cinema until it closed in 1958. The original name was restored following renovations in the early 1990s. *Special Collections and University Archives Department, University of Nevada, Reno*

One of the most interesting features of Eureka, however, can't be found above ground. William H. Clark built a two-story building on Main Street where he ran a general mercantile and hardware store downstairs. The second floor was reserved for professional offices.

In 1907, the building became the 17-room Zadow Hotel, where you could get a room — including meals and free storage for your car — for $2.50 when the Lincoln Highway came through in 1916. Four years later, it became the Eureka Hotel, and it became a Chinese restaurant around the time of World War II.

But underneath the hotel lay a whole different world. Clark built a 2.5-mile series of tunnels in response to the fires in the city, including 500-pound fireproof doors, because he was tired of seeing his merchandise go up in flames. One of the tunnels went underneath Main Street to the bank (now a pharmacy) across the way. Another led to a mansion up the hill occupied by Reinhold Sadler that served as the governor's mansion when Sadler held that office from 1896 to 1902.

A large chamber called "the Cathedral" was used as an ice room; a skylight in the chamber was used to lower merchandise from the Colonnade Hotel above. Later, the tunnels were used for less savory purposes, such as growing marijuana and as an opium den. Now, they're a favorite haunt for paranormal investigators. (With nine cemeteries in town, there might be plenty of spirits ready to do some haunting.)

This building, constructed in 1873, has housed hotels, saloons, a general store, and offices. It also sits atop a series of tunnels built to protect the store's merchandise from fire and used for a variety of purposes over the years. At left is one of the heavy metal doors used to keep the store's inventory safe. *Author photos*

Tunnels connected the bank across the street (now Economy Drug, above left), the governor's mansion, left, and the Colonnade Hotel, below. *Author photos*

The Cathedral, below, with its skylight passage to the Colonnade Hotel, right.
Author photos

Top: The Jackson House Hotel, foreground, was built in 1877, and was touted as the state's only fireproof hotel after it was burned down and rebuilt in 1880. It was known as the Brown Hotel from 1907 to 1981.

Above: This 1882 building on the south end of town started out as the Ottawa Hotel. It was a Shell gas station in the 1920s, a Union 76 station in the '40s, and a general store starting in 1967. *Author photos*

Arthur Rothstein took these views of Main Steet, Eureka, in 1940. *Library of Congress*

On the highway, 1915

"Brown's Hotel seemed to be mostly a bar room and lounging place; at least that was the impression made upon me by a glimpse I caught of the lighted room downstairs as I stood on the wooden porch. But we were shown upstairs to a very comfortable, old fashioned, high ceilinged room with heavy walnut furniture of the style of forty years ago.

"An aged, ingrain carpet was on the floor, and a wreath of wax flowers such as our grandmothers rejoiced in, hung, in deep frame, on the wall. I thought to myself that these were relics of departed glories and of a day when there was money to furnish the old hostel in the taste then in vogue...

"Eureka is a most forlorn town, perched high and dry, just as if the waves of traffic and commercial life had ebbed away and left it far up on the beach forever. They told us that it was once a big and prosperous town. But like Mariposa in California, the mining interests have been transferred to other localities, and the town is left lonely.

"As we walked along its silent and dimly lighted main strait, we saw the quaint wooden porches in front of the shops and houses, some high, some low, making an uneven sidewalk. Practically all of the shows were closed, only the saloons being open."

Effie Price Gladding
Across the Continent by the Lincoln Highway

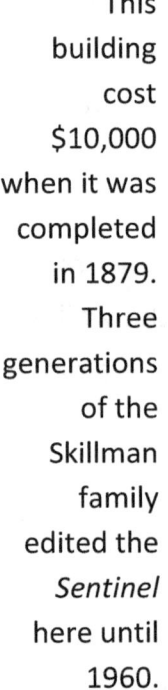

This building cost $10,000 when it was completed in 1879. Three generations of the Skillman family edited the *Sentinel* here until 1960.

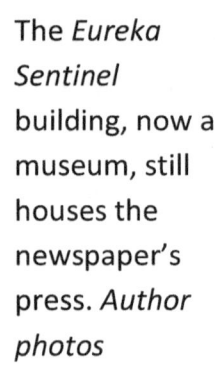

The *Eureka Sentinel* building, now a museum, still houses the newspaper's press. *Author photos*

The plaque at right was mounted along the Lincoln Highway outside of town by General Motors and later moved next to the courthouse.

An original Lincoln Highway marker sits outside the Eureka County Courthouse, an impressive structure built in 1879. *Author photos*

Top: The Tannehill pine log cabin, at top, was built just south of town on the highway around 1864. Occupied by the Tannehill brothers for about a year before they sold their mining interests, it's believed to have been the first dwelling in the area.

Above: This façade is all that's left of a building on Main Street.
Author photos

Garages were a necessity along the highway in the days before cars were as reliable as they are today. The 1940 photo at top from the Historical American Building Survey shows the Hooper Garage on Spring Street. The author photo above shows a faded motor oil ad on the highway in Eureka.

The pharmacy at left once housed the Farmers and Merchants Bank, founded by Edna C. Plummer, which moved there in the 1930s. The bank tellers' cage was converted into a pharmacy counter. Plummer was not only the first woman to ever found a national bank, she also became the first woman in the nation to serve as district attorney (for Eureka County in 1918). The site once was home to "The Corner! The Finest Saloon in the State." The Raine's Market building, constructed in 1880, housed Eureka Drug and Fountain from the 1940s to 1978, while another section of the building was home to the Kitchen Brothers' Market from 1929 to 1972. The Owl Saloon at right is housed in a building that dates to 1930 and was home to the Nevada Club in the 1940s and '50s. It's said to be haunted by the ghost of a prostitute who was stabbed by a rival in the 1870s.
Author photos

Louie's Lounge operated in a stone building that started out as a dry goods store founded by two Jewish merchants back in 1874.

The former Lincoln Hotel on Main Street (shown from front and rear) has seen better days. Three buildings were combined to form the Lincoln, with more than 50 rooms, in 1941. Lee and Blanche Olinger bought the establishment in 1946, and Blanche Olinger was strangled to death there in 1968, resulting in a sensational trial. The building subsequently became the Alpine Hotel and Lucky Stiff Bar, but it fell into disrepair and was condemned in 1996. *Author photos*

Eureka in 1940. *Arthur Rothstein, Library of Congress*

Finding Eureka

Location: 78 miles west of Ely

44 miles west of Hamilton

70 miles east of Austin

Route: U.S. 50 runs along Main Street, which is also called the Lincoln Highway through town. The oldest Lincoln alignment branches off west of the highway along County Road 101 to Eureka Canyon. A slightly newer alignment meanders through town east of the highway along West Robbins Street, Nob Hill Avenue, Sheridan Street, Ridgetop Road, and Sheridan Street again.

Lincoln Highway, Austin.
Author photo

U.S. 50 outside Austin. *Author photo*

The loneliest Road in America

Eureka to Austin

Once you leave Eureka, the next stop is Austin. There's not much between the two towns except for wide-open spaces. The 1918 *Automobile Blue Book* mentioned stone ruins about 25 miles out of Eureka and a ranch with a corral a little more than six miles from Austin, but that was it.

Early motorists faced a challenge driving up to Hickison Summit on a stretch of the Lincoln Highway called "Ford's Defeat" — so named because many a Model T met her match there. Fortunately, a rancher in the area was there to provide a helping hand. For a price, that is. He would help motorists who couldn't (literally) make the grade by offering a team of horses to pull them the rest of the way.

Ford's Defeat was regraded in the 1930s, with the new alignment offering a less strenuous journey up the mountains.

Hickison Summit is also noteworthy for its nearby petroglyphs, rock carvings that date back some 10,000 years that were produced by the Western Shoshone who hunted in the area. Interestingly, the summit's name is a misspelling: It's located on the road to a ranch that was owned by John Hickerson.

Burros that escaped from miners and ranchers in the '40s can sometimes be seen in this area, between the petroglyphs and Toquima Cave.

Getting There

Directions from the 1913 Lincoln Highway directory, with miles between each entry, beginning about 5 miles from Austin:

0 miles: Ford small creek; probably dry in summer.

0.3 mile: Caution for steep descent.

0.1 mile: Six-mile house.

0.1 mile: Culvert over creek; probably dry in summer.

0.2 mile: Fine view of desert mountains on right.

0.5 mile: Road in from left at sign-post. Beginning of second ascent.

0.7 mile: Water trough on right.

0.7 mile: Summit, 9,000 feet. Caution for steep descent.

On the highway, 1915

"…two women reached my hilltop, the older one driving the Ford car in which they were traveling… The women warned us that in the valley at the foot of the hill was a very bad mud hole which we must inevitably negotiate. They said that a stream from the mountains had in a recent freshet overflowed the plain and reduced both the road and the adjoining country to the state of a swamp.

"They assured us that we simply must go through the mud hole and that we were bound to get stuck in it. They cheered us, however, by telling us that a nearby settler had a sturdy draught horse and that he would in all probability pull us out for the sum of $2.00 a motor car…

"[When the Ford started through the mud hole], its wheels sank immediately, and no turning on of power could push it forward. We then shouted to the settler. He came across the field with a big horse… I was secretly glad that the poor fellow who had so recently cast his lot in this lonely and immense valley had a chance to earn some ready money."

Effie Price Gladding,
Across the Continent the Lincoln Highway

Desert storms such as this one can flash across the barren landscape between Eureka and Austin on U.S. 50. *Author photo*

On the highway, 1918

"Fair to good road with stretches of natural gravel. Owing to scarcity of water and uninhabited country, the tourist is cautioned to take on full supplies at Austin, as no gas, oil or food may be obtained on the route."

Automobile Blue Book, Vol. 8

On the highway, 1923

"Natural prairie trail except 12 miles of good graded mountain road approaching Austin... After storms or prolonged dry spells better going will be found in the hills and high places than on the flats... The country is uninhabited save for a few ranches along the way."

Automobile Blue Book, Vol. 4

Austin

County: Lander *(county seat, 1862-1979)*
Elevation: 6,594
Established: 1862
Unincorporated

1916
    Population: 700
    Accommodations 3 hotels, camp site
    Features: 3 garages, bank, 20 general businesses

2022
    Population: 167 (2020)
    Features: Café, service station, historic churches

You wouldn't know it to look at it, but Austin was once the second-largest city in Nevada. Named after Austin, Texas, hometown to one of its founders, it reached its population peak in 1863, at 7,000, a year after (legend says) a Pony Express rider discovered silver there. The discovery led to the founding of other mining towns in the region, including Belmont and Ione, both now ghost towns to the south.

Today, Austin itself is a living ghost town. It shipped some $50 million worth of gold and silver in the next decade before the pace began to wane and the town entered a slow but steady decline that's lasted a century and a half. In recent years, even some of its more modern businesses have closed up shop.

As of 2022, the Champs gas station on the western edge of town was still open to greet travelers, serving burgers out of a food truck in the parking lot. The Cozy Comfort Motel had been refurbished, and its owners had opened Grandma's for breakfast and dinner down the street. But elsewhere, boarded-up windows and vacant storefronts greet motorists passing through.

AMERICA'S LONELIEST ROAD

Top: Austin in 1868, with Austin Methodist Church, dedicated two years earlier, in the distance. *Timothy H. O'Sullivan, Smithsonian Institution*

Above: Overview of Austin today, with Austin Methodist Church at left and Lander County Courthouse at center left. *Author photo*

The Lincoln Motel, named for the highway, sits silent and unoccupied.

The Pony Express gas station is permanently closed.

The Golden Club, where Clara Williams dealt blackjack for years after her husband passed away in 1966, still has the sign out front, but the doors are locked and have been that way for years. A former hotel next door is nothing more than a triple-arched façade.

Austin still boasts four impressive church buildings… for a population of barely 150. Only one of them still holds services. Its large auto garage sits long empty. It even has a "castle" just outside town that sits unoccupied behind a barbed-wire fence.

The town has a historic hotel that no longer functions as one, operating only as a café with limited hours. The International opened in 1860 as a one-story building more than 150 miles away in Virginia City. Its wooden section was dismantled three years later and moved to Austin, where it was put back together, while a new six-story hotel by the same name was erected on the original site. (The International in Virginia City was the state's tallest building at six stories until it was lost in a 1914 fire).

A lot of the buildings in Austin have been there a very long time, and nearly as many of them are vacant or closed. But there's plenty of history in Austin, if you know where to look. As you enter town from Eureka, you may notice the Gridley Store, once run by an unsuccessful candidate for mayor who gained more fame by losing than he ever could have if he'd won.

In losing, way back in 1864, Reuel Colt Gridley also lost a bet that required him to carry a 50-pound sack of flour from one end of town to the other. The entire town turned out to watch. When he was done, Gridley didn't know what to do with the flour, so he had it auctioned off, with the money going to the Sanitary Fund, an organization that was working to help wounded Civil War soldiers. (It later became the Red Cross.)

Word of the auction spread, and other communities invited Gridley to conduct similar auctions — which, when all was said and done, raised $275,000 for the charity. Unfortunately for Gridley, his neglected store went belly-up in the meantime.

Austin was also home to Clara Crowell, who became the first woman in

Nevada to serve as sheriff in 1919 after her husband died in office, as well as to famed opera singer Emma Nevada, right. Born Emma Wixom, she was the daughter of a pioneering Austin doctor who started out singing in the Methodist Church Choir. She even sang during Gridley's "sack of flour" parade.

In 1877, she traveled to study in Vienna and sang at the coronation of England's King George V.

The proprietor of Gridley Store in Austin became famous by raising funds for wounded Civil War soldiers by carrying around a sack of flour — which was incorporated into the city's official seal. Reuel Colt Gridley raised some $275,000, but his store went bankrupt, and he died at the age of just 41. *Author photo, above*

Right: The International Hotel as it appeared in 1862 at Virginia City, before it was partially dismantled and portions of it moved to Austin. *Library of Congress*

Below: The International, no longer a hotel, on U.S. 50 in 2022. *Author photo*

Above: The International Hotel, foreground left, along Lincoln Highway in 1939. A ghost named Tommy is reputed to haunt the place, which would be spooky enough without him.

Below: Farther east on the highway, looking west, with the Austin Garage in the foreground. *Special Collections and University Archives Department, University of Nevada, Reno Nevada Reno*

Top: The Austin garage opened around 1915, but it was long closed and abandoned by the time this photo was taken in 2022.

Above: This building on U.S. 50 in Austin has been there since at least the 1930s. Both it and the garage pictured above are visible in the bottom photo on the previous page. *Author photos*

St. Augustine's Catholic Church, built in 1866, is the oldest Catholic church building in Nevada. Here it presides over two Lincoln Highway scenes, featuring the Golden Club, top, and Grandma's restaurant, above. *Author photos*

Above: Robert Hogan opened the Hotel Hogan, seen in 1940, in 1906 as part of a block of buildings that also included the Austin Café and a large store. Hogan was Lander County treasurer for 10 years beginning in 1904. *Arthur Rothstein, Library of Congress*

Right: All that's left of the hotel are its three arches. *Author photo*

Top: The Hotel Hogan, Hogan's Dry Goods, the Austin Café, and the Silver Dollar Bar on U.S. 50 in 1940. The hotel was renamed the Hotel Austin in the 1940s.

Above: Overlooking Austin in 1940. *Arthur Rothstein, Library of Congress*

Above: The Austin Firehouse, seen in 1940, was home to a hook-and-ladder company with a cart and 550 feet of rubber-lined cotton hose as early as 1886. *Arthur Rothstein, Library of Congress*

Right: The stone building has been modified to serve as a youth center. The belltower was still standing until fairly recently, but no longer is part of the structure. *Author photo*

Above: The courtroom at the Lander County Courthouse, built in 1869, was still equipped with its original potbellied stove a century later.

Right: The old city hall, built in the 1860s, sits just off the highway. *Author photos*

Above: The Magnolia Gallery and Inn building, which dates to 1864, sits next to a lodge building jointly constructed by Lander No. 8 Masonic Lodge and I.O.O.F No. 9 of Austin in 1867.

Right: The Lincoln Motel opened around 1935 but was closed as of 2022.
Author photos

Nevada's oldest bank building, constructed in 1863, became home to the town library and a saloon with a sign over the doorway welcoming "bikes, babes, [and] beer."
Author photos

The Austin Firehouse can be seen in the foreground left in this photograph displayed on the highway in town, which appears to be from the 1920s or '30s.

The same "Fireman's Block" in 1887. *Special Collections and University Archives Department, University of Nevada, Reno*

Mine developer, banker, and railroad man Anson Phelps Stokes built Stokes Castle in 1897. A replica of a tower outside Rome, it was intended as a summer home for his family, but they only visited twice, spending a little more than a month there, before Stokes sold his interests in the area and left town.
Author photo

Finding Austin

Location: 70 miles west of Eureka

119 miles east of Fallon

Route: U.S. 50 and the Lincoln Highway are the main street through town. An earlier alignment of the Lincoln runs along Forest Road 43003 just before you hit Austin from the east.

Headstones and an angel statue watching over a grave at the Austin Cemetery, founded in 1863. It was placed on the National Register of Historic Places in 2003.
Author photo

U.S. 50 between Austin and Fallon.
Author photo

Just west of Austin on U.S. Highway 50.
Author photo

The loneliest Road in America

Austin to Fallon

Once you leave Austin and head toward Fallon, you begin to fully realize you're in the desert. On this stretch of road, you'll encounter a giant sand mountain and long stretches of alkali flats that were among the most difficult for early road-builders to traverse. If you take a detour on a now-bypassed version of the Lincoln Highway, however, you'll encounter perhaps the most beautiful scenery you'll find along the U.S. 50 corridor.

Between Austin and Fallon, you'll also find the ruins of an old Pony Express station, an odd sight called the Shoe Tree, and Middlegate Station, where they serve up some delicious burgers. There are more Pony Express ruins at Cold Springs Station, a reminder that U.S. 50 and the Lincoln Highway before it closely followed the old Pony Express route, which followed the Central Overland Trail through Nevada.

The Pony Express was an ambitious concept that involved riders carrying mail in a 2,000-mile relay across the western United States from St. Joseph, Missouri, to Sacramento beginning in April of 1860. Each rider would travel about 75 miles (a 24-hour journey) before delivering his saddlebag to the next in line. Swing stations were situated every 10 or 15 miles to allow the riders to dismount and climb aboard a fresh horse.

"There were about eighty pony riders in the saddle all the time, night and day, stretching in a long, scattering procession from Missouri to California," Mark Twain wrote in 1872, "forty flying eastward, and forty toward the west, and among them making four hundred gallant horses earn a stirring livelihood and see a deal of scenery every single day of the year."

For all its enduring fame, the Pony Express only operated for a year and a half, giving way to more efficient telegraph operations. The ruins of a few old stations on the Central Overland Route, however, are still visible today along the highway in Nevada.

The New Pass Overland Station, top, and Cold Springs Station, above, both operated in the 1860s on this stretch of what would one day be the Lincoln Highway and U.S. 50. *Author photos*

Top: An eastbound mileage sign in 1940 shows the distance to Austin, Eureka, and Salt Lake City. *Arthur Rothstein, Library of Congress.*
Above: New Pass Canyon between Austin and Alpine Ranch was the original route for the Lincoln Highway and is the current route for U.S. 50. *University of Michigan Special Collections Research Center*

This stretch of highway is also home to three "gates," (so named because they were placed at cuts in the mountains), each of which initially served as stops on the Overland Stage Route, as well. One of them, Eastgate, was along State Route 722, the scenic version of Lincoln Highway and U.S. 50 in use from roughly 1925 to 1967.

Hairpin curves looking west, just west of Carroll Summit. *Author photo*

On the highway, 1916

"Williams ranch belongs to Williams' estate, Nevada. Mr. Williams' son says that 20 miles from here is a miniature Grand Canyon of Colorado, which is almost identical to the larger canyon of Arizona and equally as beautiful. He suggests that tourists make inquiry any time it permits and that this detour be made."

The Complete Official Road Guide of the Lincoln Highway

The above description is an apt one. State Route 722 is worth the detour for the canyon alone, where you're likely to find cattle grazing leisurely in the afternoon sun. But along the way you also might find yourself face-to-face with bighorn sheep, either crossing the road or staring down at you from one of the impressive rock formations that line the old highway.

The route was originally adopted because it was shorter than the once-and-future route through New Pass to the north, but was ultimately relegated to state highway status because its hairpin curves couldn't accommodate the big rigs that increasingly used the road.

Bighorn sheep can be seen beside State Route 722 west of Carroll Summit, and they aren't shy about crossing the road, either. *Author photos*

The view from the Carroll Summit is breathtaking as you stare west down at the winding road that stretches away from you through the mountains.

Carroll itself was "a live and thriving mining camp" after Charlie Carroll struck a vein of ore there in 1911, but it didn't last long. Today, all that's left is an old, abandoned Texaco station. When the highway was moved to the Carroll route in 1925, a small building was brought in from Lake Tahoe to serve travelers there. In addition to gas pumps, the building contained a store, café, and bar. The station remained open until the route was switched back to New Pass Canyon in the 1960s, around the same time Eastgate's store and Chevron gas stop was shuttered.

This picturesque canyon west of Carroll Summit has been described as a miniature Grand Canyon. *Author photo*

Carroll Summit

Top: Cattle meander along the roadside east of Carroll Summit, overlooking the valley below. **Above:** Impressive rock formations line the highway near the summit. *Author photos*

Above: Carroll Summit, looking west.

Left: Curves on State Route 722, the former Lincoln Highway, carry travelers up the hill west of Carroll Summit. *Author photos*

Top: The Texaco station near Carroll Summit is seen around 1950 in this vintage postcard. *Special Collections and University Archives Department, University of Nevada, Reno.*

Above: The station sits abandoned today. *Author photo*

Eastgate

Eastgate was laid out as a full-fledged community in 1906, and a feeling of optimism filled the air. Already, it was reported, "there are more than 500 people at East Gate and there is a continuous stream of people going in. New businesses are being erected in a night, and an air of prosperity pervades everything." More than 250 lots had been sold at prices of $100 for corner lots and $50 for interior lots. The fledgling town had two saloons, a restaurant (with several more in the works, a butcher shop, and a soon-to-open general store. The 1916 *Complete Official Road Guide* described it as "a fine place to stop" that offered travelers "meals, lodging, gas, oil, drinking water, radiator water, [and a] camp site." At an altitude of 5,291 feet, it was on the road coming down out of the mountains. Today, it consists of a ranch and a few ruins on State Route 722.
Author photo

Top: Eastgate Station's store offered Chevron gas at an altitude of 5,291 feet on State Route 722 coming down out of the mountains on the western slope. Today, it consists of a ranch and a few ruins. *Courtesy of the Churchill County Museum, Bill and Bunny Corkill Collection*

Above: Eastgate Station in 2022. *Author photo*

The Shoe Tree a couple of miles east of Middlegate has an interesting story behind it. According to legend, a couple was traveling east on U.S. 50 after being married when they got into an argument and the man told his bride to walk home. He later thought better of it, they reconciled, and lived happily ever after. Each year, they would toss a pair of shoes onto this tree to reaffirm their love. That tree was cut down in 2011, but the tradition lives on with a new tree, shown here. *Author photos*

Middlegate

The bar and motel at Middlegate Station. *Author photos*

Not much happened at Middlegate after the Pony Express era, at least not until 1942, when Ida Ferguson bought the land from the Bureau of Land Management at auction. Today, there's a bar, restaurant, and convenience store there, alongside an old motel. The eatery is known for its Monster Burgers, and visitors will notice the ceiling's covered with dollar bills bearing the names of customers who've eaten there. The owner said they were left there for future visits because there wasn't a nearby bank. Middlegate is a few hundred yards off U.S. 50 to the south on the road to Gabbs, Berlin, and Ione, but the old Lincoln Highway, above, runs by right out front. *Author photos*

Detour: Ione

Ione, "the town that refused to die," arose from the mining fever that began in Austin. It was the site of Nye County's first courthouse in 1864, although it remained the county seat for just three years. It's about 53 miles to the south and a little west of Austin. Turn south at Middlegate Station. *Author photos*

Detour: Berlin

The remains of milling operations in Berlin are seen here. The ghost town, which was established in 1897, lies nearly 60 miles away in the same direction as Ione. Like Ione, it owed its existence to the mining craze that spread from Austin. It was all but deserted by 1911, but the fossils of about 40 aquatic dinosaurs called Ichthyosaurs were found nearby starting in 1928, and a state park was established there. *Author photos*

Westgate

Eastgate, Middlegate, and Westgate were all originally Pony Express stations. A town plat was filed for Westgate in 1907, but the community never took off. It was the site of some mining activity and, during the Depression, a Civilian Conservation Corps camp. But today, there's just a windmill, some brickwork, and a very small marker to indicate anything was ever there.
Author photos

Frenchman's Station

Frenchman's Station isn't there anymore, but it was around for a long time, serving as an important way station between Austin and Fallon on the Lincoln Highway and, later, U.S. 50. "Frenchy" Bermond, a Frenchman (naturally) founded it as a stagecoach stop just east of the salt flats in 1904. The Postal Service, which operated a post office there from 1920 to 1926, called it Bermond. Frenchman Station offered a hotel, and Bermond served up food in his highly rated restaurant. But the most important commodity in this part of the desert was water, which Bermond had trucked in and sold to travelers. He built a holding tank with a sign that read, "If you don't want to pay for this water, leave it alone." *University of Michigan Special Collections Research Center*

Frenchy Bermond died in 1926, but his station endured until 1985. That's when the owners of the property deeded it to the Navy, which was using nearby Dixie Valley as a bombing range. The buildings, seen here in the late 1940s, were demolished two years later. *Special Collections and University Archives Department, University of Nevada, Reno*

On the highway, 1915

"In Nevada, two important problems to be solved are the flats around Frenchman station and at Sand Springs. These sections should be taken care of at an early date, and if these flats can not be sklered, efforts should be made to put a stone foundation in the most serious spots. This locality, which is not long, looms up tremendously for the tourist by contrast, for the rest of the road across Nevada is splendid, and the scenic attractions are not surpassed anywhere on the entire route."

George A. Briggs
***Reno Evening Gazette*, Oct. 11, 1915**

Left: Heading toward Middlegate on U.S. 50.

Above and right: Sand Mountain is a 300-foot-high dune about 20 miles east of Fallon that was formed by wind from the deposits of Lake Lahontan, a body of water that covered much of the state until about 10,000 years ago. Today, it attracts dune buggy enthusiasts. *Author photos*

On the highway, 1915

"We passed Frenchman's Flat, where there was a little restaurant and where a Frenchman came out to pass the time of day. He greeted us very pleasantly and would doubtless have given us a good meal if we had not already had one."

Effie Price Gladding
Across the Continent by the Lincoln Highway

"Five hours of honest toil were spent, extricating the car from the mud."

Thomas J.H. O'Shaughnessy
Rambles on Overland Trails

On the highway, 1916

"From Fallon east, as far as Austin, 115 miles, the chief difficulties in improving this road are encountered. ... From Salt Wells to Sand Springs, twelve miles, is the worst section of the road. It runs across two flats, known as the Eight Mile and Four Mile flat, which become practically a quagmire in the winter."

W.H. Lynch and H.E. Stewart
Report of Inspection of the Lincoln Highway
from Reno to Ely, Nevada

On the highway, 1923

"Natural prairie road to Sand Springs, then 18 miles of gravel highway across salt and alkali flats; last 12 miles sandy dirt... Water is scarce and supplies should be replenished at every opportunity. Good meals, accommodations and supplies at Frenchman's Station."

Automobile Blue Book, Vol. 4

Top: The Fallon Flats or Fallon Sink was a treacherous area for travelers in 1915. *University of Michigan Special Collections Research Center*

Above: Travel in the area is a lot smoother today. *Author photo*

A new grade across the Fallon Sink, not yet graveled, is shown between Sand Springs and Salt Wells in 1920. The "Fallon Mud Flats" was described in the *Reno Evening Gazette* as "practically impassable" and "probably... the poorest stretch of the Lincoln Highway across the entire United States." But a new 12-mile section of level roadway, graded up from 3 to 6 feet and surfaced with crushed rock and packed gravel, opened in the summer of 1922. The road, on a 20-foot-wide grade, included 18-foot turnouts every 2,000 feet. *University of Michigan Special Collections Research Center*

Above: Various travelers have stopped to arrange rocks on the Fallon Flats into images and messages alongside U.S. 50. Among them is the entire preamble to the U.S. Constitution, measuring 500 yards long and created by Washington, D.C. resident Mike Iacovone in 2017. The message was still visible five years later, when this photo was taken.

Right: An RV Dump sign marks the site of Salt Wells. *Author photos*

Stillwater

Main Street in Stillwater, as it appeared in 1907. By that time, only about 30 residents remained in the town which was once the seat of Churchill County. It had a post office by 1865, and today consists of nothing more than a few scattered homes and farm fields. Stillwater straddled the second version of the Lincoln Highway, a detour around the Fallon Sink from Westgate to Fallon called the Stillwater Cutoff. It wound its way down into Fallon along what's still called Stillwater Street today (although part of it is a dirt road that's on private property. It wasn't long, however, before the Lincoln Highway was rerouted through the Sink again, this time on a better road. Although it had been a Pony Express stop, Stillwater wasn't on U.S. 50 when it came through, and it remained a sleepy little town for the remainder of its existence before drifting off into the realm of memory. Its brick hotel, built in 1907, came down after World War II, its post office closed in 1959, and its store burned in 1963. Public pools that opened in the early '20 closed by the early '70s.

Stillwater School is one of the few significant buildings remaining from the former town. The school, which had two classrooms (for grades 1-4 and 5-8), was completed in 1918. It's similar to a school that opened in Hazen the same year, with the two districts coordinating their efforts. The building still stands on a curve in the highway at 11417 Stillwater Road. Graduations were held there until 1956.
Author photos

The Churchill County Courthouse, built in 1903, sits on U.S. 50 at U.S. 95 (Maine Street) in Fallon. *Author photo*

Fallon

County: Churchill *(county seat)*
Elevation: 6,594
Established: 1896
Incorporated: 1908

1916

Population: 1,200

Accommodations 2 hotels

Features: 3 garages, 2 newspapers, bank, telegraph company

2022

Population: 8,645 (2019)

Features: High school, churches, casinos, numerous businesses

Getting There

Selected directions from the 1913 Lincoln Highway directory, with miles between each entry, from Sand Springs:

0 miles: On the edge of salt flat. (Note. — Built-up road across flat — is impassable in wet weather.

0.3 mile: Deep sand; road from here on skirts flat on hill side to northeast.

16.3 miles: Cross bridge toward tree.

1.3 miles: Turn right crossing bridge over canal; leaving poles. Now between two canals.

6.7 miles: Swing left and right across bridge; bearing right, then turning left across bridge over large canal, again bearing left over another bridge and follow poles; wire fence on right.

1.0 mile: Turn right at bridge and waterfall on left; follow six wire poles on left.

1.4 miles: Right and left turn around stables.

Fallon is called "the Oasis of Nevada," and after passing through the desert lands to the east, it probably seems like exactly that. Not to say it's cool, though: The average temperature tops 100 in July and rises above 98 in August, while June and September are nearly as hot.

The town is named for Mike Fallon a local rancher who moved to the area in 1896 and opened a post office at a crossroads, but Native Americans in the area called it Jim's Town in honor of Jim Richards, who opened a general store on Fallon's land.

After Theodore Roosevelt targeted the Lahontan Valley for the first project under the Reclamation Act of 1902, Richards sold his land to Warren Williams, for whom the main street through town is named. (Maine Street is Maine, rather than Main, because that was Williams' home state.)

Williams heard opportunity knock, and he answered.

Fallon wrested the county seat from Stillwater. It benefited from the completion of Lahontan Dam, which brought electricity into town in 1914, though the city never grew to the 20,000 residents once projected. Today, it's about half that. The Maine Street Historic District includes a number of buildings on or just off the highway that were built in the first two decades of the 20th century.

If you're driving in from the east into Fallon, though, you can't get there on the old Lincoln Highway. The 1913 route runs straight through the Fallon Naval Air Station before emerging at the west side as State Route 720. The station was built in 1942 and is still in use today.

A later alignment of the highway skirts the air base to the south on Nevada Route 119 before turning north on NV 115, where it rejoins the older highway just southeast of town.

Right: A jet marks Fallon NAS along U.S. 50.

Below: The air station's west gate, where the old Lincoln Highway enters the base. *Author photos*

This now-closed service station sits in a once-prime location at a bend in the road where the first and second alignments of the Lincoln Highway meet at Stillwater Road. *Author photo*

From there, you curve into town at Stillwater Street, take East Street for two blocks north to Center, then follow Center for three blocks west to Maine Street. On the south side of Center, you'll pass the old Fallon Garage, which dates to 1923 and a century later is chock-full of vintage memorabilia, including historic autos and old gas pumps. Across the street is the Overland Hotel, which is even older, dating to 1908.

The Overland was a boarding house for Basque stockmen in its heyday.

On Maine, you'll find such landmarks as the Fallon Theatre, which opened in 1920 as the Rex and took on its current name a decade later when it was purchased by the owners of cinemas in Ely and McGill. The theater originally seated 1,150 patrons, including 300 in a balcony, and featured a $20,000 organ to accompany its silent films.

Maine will take you to Williams Street, aka U.S. 50, which joins the old Lincoln Highway at an intersection that features the 1903 county courthouse on one corner and the Fallon Nugget on another. (Every county seat from Ely in the east to Carson City in the west is along U.S. 50 and the Lincoln Highway.)

Above: The Overland Hotel and Saloon operated a casino beginning in 1945 but discontinued gaming in 1954.

Left: A section of the old highway, formerly part of Stillwater Road, enters private property.
Author photos

The Fallon Garage and its collection of vintage vehicles and gas pumps. *Author photos*

STOP! at Fallon, Nevada and see UNCLE SAM'S $9,000,000.00 FARM. Also the great LAHONTAN DAM. The entrance to the desert from the west; The end of the desert from the east. A REAL LIVE CITY.

FALLON GARAGE

Geo. C. Coverston, Prop.   Phone 881

Repairs of all kinds including lathe work, vulcanizing, recharging storage batteries and Prest-O-Welding. Storage in a Fire Proof Garage. Complete stock of tires and tubes, in fact everything for the Automobile.

Information Cheerfully Given

Top: The 1920 Gray-Reid & Co. commercial block at Maine and Center streets has housed a variety of retail stores over the years, including J.C. Penney, Safeway, Fallon Mercantile, and Sprouse-Reitz. Gray-Reid was a Reno-based department store founded by Joseph H. Gray and Hosea E. Reid in the early 20th century.

Above: A billboard on a nearby Maine Street building advertises Selz Shoes, a company that flourished from the 19th century through the 1920s. *Author photos*

Fallon had a bustling downtown back in the day, with businesses such as the Barrel House Bar and Café, Western Hotel, Sagebrush Café, and Owl Club lining Maine Street. *The Lincoln Highway Collection of Russell Rein*

Fallon along Maine Street in the late 1930s. *Special Collections and University Archives Department, University of Nevada, Reno*

Finding Fallon

Location: 119 miles west of Austin, 15 miles east of Hazen

The route: Portions of Stillwater, East, Center, Maine, and Williams avenues

Fallon's Maine Street in the late 1940s. *Special Collections and University Archives Department, University of Nevada, Reno*

This vintage postcard shows Maine Street lined with casinos including the Palace Club, foreground, which operated from 1939 to 1967. The Fallon Nugget, seen in a smaller space here, now occupies that site. *Author collection*

Left: The Fallon Theatre opened in 1920 as the Rex.

Below: The *Fallon Eagle* newspaper building in 2022, occupied by a bail bonds business and glass shop. The *Eagle* was founded in 1907 and merged with the *Churchill Standard* (founded in 1904) in 1958 to become the *Fallon Eagle-Standard*. It is published twice a week, on Wednesdays and Fridays. *Author photos*

The Fallon Nugget, above, at U.S. 50 and 95 (Maine and Williams) opened in 1963. At the time, it was one of several casinos lining the west side of Maine Street on the same block. Others included the Owl Club and Sagebrush Club, both of which opened in 1931, the year gambling was legalized in Nevada. The Palace Club, which opened in 1939, originally occupied the site where the Nugget now stands. It lasted until 1967. These days, most of the casinos in Fallon, such as the Depot, left, which opened in 1987, can be found along U.S. 50. *Author photos*

The old dirt section of the Lincoln Highway at left can be found not far from the newer section, below, which runs by the rear of Stockman's Casino The casino, which fronts U.S. 50, opened in 1960 and features 10,000 square feet of gaming space, making it large in comparison to other local gambling halls. *Author photos*

Lincoln Highway route on west side of Washoe Valley. *Author photo*

U.S. 50 near Dayton.
Author photo

The loneliest Road in America

Fallon to Carson City

The road between Fallon and Carson City is actually two roads. The split began on the Lincoln Highway and was followed when U.S. 50 replaced it.

Originally, the Lincoln Highway branched off northwest from Fallon and headed to downtown Reno, where it split in two: One branch kept going west, while the other took a hard turn south through the Washoe Valley to Carson City. But that changed in the 1920s, when the split was moved east to Leeteville, a little west of Fallon.

The Reno-bound portion of the highway continued up through Truckee and the Donner Pass north of Lake Tahoe, while the southern branch ran along the south side of the lake and through the Sierra Nevada, rejoining its sister route in Sacramento. The northern branch was known as the Donner Route, while the southern alternative was dubbed the Pioneer Route.

When the federal highway system came along in 1926, the split was preserved. The Pioneer Route was designated as U.S. 50, while the Donner Route was U.S. 50 Alternate from Fallon to Fernley; onward from there, it was numbered as U.S. 40.

The old north-south segment between Reno and Carson through the Washoe Valley, meanwhile, became part of the new U.S. 395.

A road sign heading east shows where U.S. 50 and its alternate route come together at Leeteville Junction, a few miles west of Fallon. A post office, named for the first postmistress, Esther Leete, opened in 1895, and a townsite was laid out but never developed. An earlier settlement on the site called Ragtown was in existence as a "collection of tents and canvass [sic] shanties" that offered food, whiskey, and gambling. It grew to a population of 200 but was wiped out in a flood 10 years later. *Author photo*

On the highway, 1916

"From Reno to Fallon the road, as far as the Washoe County line, thirty-nine miles, is in good condition, as it follows the abandoned grade of the Southern Pacific company practically all the way... The section in Churchill county, as far as Fallon, twenty-five miles, while not in good condition at present, could be made so at a very moderate cost by the use of a road grader and drag in the spring when the road is wet, and by the installation of several culverts."

W.H. Lynch and H.E. Stewart
Report of Inspection of the Lincoln Highway
from Reno to Ely, Nevada

This monument is all that's left of Ragtown, which got its name from the pioneer laundry that was spread over bushes in the area. Asa Kenyon founded a trading post on the site in 1954. *Author photo*

The Donner Route

The Donner Route was named for Donner Pass, which in turn had been named for the ill-fated Donner Party, many of whom perished in the winter of 1846-47, caught in the Sierra Nevada snows.

The advantage of this route, which was the original course followed by the Lincoln Highway, is that it went through the state's largest city at the time, Reno. Before it got there, it passed through such towns as Hazen, Fernley, Wadsworth, and, finally, Sparks.

Wadsworth is little more than a bend in the road today, but in 1916, it was the largest community between Ely and Reno, with a population of more than 1,300 people. Sparks was nearly twice as large at 2,500, but it wasn't on the original route, which bypassed the town completely to the south. (That omission was rectified to include Sparks on the highway two years after the original highway was laid out.)

After passing through Reno, it headed toward Verdi and the California state line before reaching Truckee, north of Lake Tahoe.

What looks like an old depot sign is affixed atop a roof in Hazen. *Author photo*

Hazen

County: Churchill
Elevation: 4,006
Established: 1903 as Southern Pacific Railroad station
Unincorporated

1916

    Population: 100

    Accommodations: Hotel, camp site

    Features: Garage, 8 general businesses, public school

2022

    Population: Handful of residents

Hazen is known as the place where Nevada's last hanging occurred. It didn't happen on a scaffold. An ex-con and former saloon owner named William "Nevada Red" Wood was strung up from a telegraph pole on February 27, 1905.

Wood operated a saloon with a partner serving men working to build Derby Dam, between Wadsworth and Sparks, but he'd been forced to quit the area after the partner died mysteriously late in 1904. He was soon in trouble again, arrested for armed robbery of a saloon in Reno and possession of opium, but he managed to beat the rap when the robbery victim refused to testify.

"There is no doubt but what 'Red' Wood was a hard man," the *Reno Evening Gazette* reported. "He had operated at Derby and is said to have been a leader of the thugs and cutthroats that made of that place a hellhole of crime."

Next, he made his way to Hazen, where he and another man tried to rob some laborers near the depot. The robbery went awry, however, when the station agent fired a shotgun; Wood's partner in crime escaped, but Wood himself was captured and placed in a wooden jail cell.

Wood was set for trial, but a lynch mob broke into the cell overnight while the constable was asleep in the hotel he owned next door. After breaking down the door with an axe, they hauled Wood out to the telegraph pole, where he was strung up and left to die.

Hazen's post office opened in 1904, and it had a school and hotel in addition to the depot. The heart of the town, however, went up in flames in 1908. The post office continued to operate until 1978, and you can still find a couple of stores by the roadside there. But don't bother knocking on the door. They're closed, from the looks of it, permanently.

Finding Hazen

Location: 15 miles west of Fallon
19 miles east of Hazen
Route: Old Lincoln Highway, Reno Highway

Hazen businesses stand beside the highway, but they were closed when they were photographed on this day in 2022. The Hazen Store, top, was built in 1944 after an earlier store was torn down when the highway was realigned. Part of the building is as old as the town itself, dating to 1904, when it operated at another location as Shorty's Bar. *Author photos*

A sign visible from the highway proclaims that "it's happening in Hazen," but it's unclear exactly what "it" is. *Author photo*

Hazen, seen in the summer of 1905, was founded two years earlier as a tent city for workers on the Newlands Irrigation Project. *Public domain*

Fernley garage in the 1930s. *Special Collections and University Archives Department, University of Nevada, Reno*

Fernley

County: Lyon

Elevation: 4,160

Established: 1904

Incorporated: 2001

1916

    Population: 100

    Accommodations: Lodging, meals, camp site

    Features: 4 general businesses, public school

2022

    Population: 21,476 (2019)

Finding Fernley

Location: 19 miles west of Hazen

             3 miles southeast of Wadsworth

Route: Farm District Road, Cottonwood, U.S. 50 Alternate

The Fernley Underpass along the Lincoln Highway and U.S. 50 Alternate was built in the 1930s. *Author photo*

No one knows why Fernley is called Fernley. Like other communities in the area, it attracted workers to the Newlands Irrigation Project, which was finished in 1905, and later, settlers who could make use of the water it provided. A post office and school both opened in 1908, and two years later, the town was home to 159 residents.

The Lincoln Highway came through in 1913, running along a route south of today's U.S. 50 Alternate today that follows Farm District Road and Cottonwood Lane.

Fernley remained a relatively small, rural town for much of its existence. It had just 654 residents in 1960, before the Nevada Cement Company came to town and helped kickstart growth. Most of its residents have arrived since 2000, when its population was just over 5,000, about one-quarter of what it was two decades later.

The Fernley schoolhouse is pictured in 1913, the same year the Lincoln Highway was established. *City of Fernley, Creative Commons 3.0*

The Fernley area was known to early travelers for being at the southern end of a treacherous, barren wasteland called the 40-Mile Desert. The California Emigrant Trail (and later the Victory Highway), traversed this desert, and pioneers passed this way from 1843 until the end of the 1860s.

There were two separate routes, but whichever way you took, you'd need to travel 40 miles without water. One took you to the Truckee River near Ragtown, and the other met the river near Wadsworth. It took two days to get across, and many travelers didn't make it — even though they typically traveled at night to avoid the heat of the sun. In fact, nearly 1,000 people died trying to cross the desert before 1850 alone, and 10 times that many animals perished.

The desert made such an impression on Mark Twain that he wrote about it in stark terms.

U.S. 50 passes along the southern edge of the 40-Mile Desert, the most feared segment of the California Emigrant Trail. *Author photo*

"It was a dreary pull and a long and thirsty one, for we had no water," Twain wrote of his own experience. "From one extremity of this desert to the other, the road was white with the bones of oxen and horses. It would hardly be an exaggeration to say that we could have walked the forty miles and set our feet on a bone at every step!"

A marker along the Carson Route, which passed through Ragtown, carries the ominous headline "To Rot and Rust" along with a quote from traveler Pusey Graves dated to 1850: "Daylight revealed to my eyes the awful sight of dead horses and cattle lying in heaps. ... And O my country! The wagons and stoves and trunks of property of all kinds that was left to rot and rust in the desert."

The Lincoln Highway, marked by a monument at left, followed Farm District Road in Fernley, below. *Author photos*

Joy and Larry's Café served truck drivers and others passing through Fernley in the 1930s. *Special Collections and University Archives Department, University of Nevada, Reno*

Wadsworth

County: Washoe
Elevation: 4,079
Established: 1868
Unincorporated

1916

    Population: 1,309

    Accommodations: 3 hotels, campsite

    Features: 4 garages, 3 general business places, 2 schools

2022

    Population: 834 (2010)

    Features: Historic church, pizza parlor

Wadsworth was once a thriving railroad community with hotels like the Columbus, saloons, and stores. It was Washoe County's largest town in the 1870s, thanks in no small measure to its role as a key supply depot for the Central Pacific Railroad. In the 1870s, it was Washoe County's biggest town, boasting a 20-stall railroad roundhouse and machine shops.

An impressive two-story schoolhouse was built in 1896, but just past the turn of the century, the Central Pacific line bypassed Wadsworth and shifted its focus to Sparks. Still, there were three hotels and four garages there in 1916, when the population stood at more than 1,300.

The post office, established in 1868, is still open. Wadsworth was also the site of the Triangle River Ranch brothel, which opened on June 3, 1955. Its owner, Joe Conforte, who would later open the more famous Mustang Ranch brothel nearby, ran a bare-bones operation with two employees.

"There were no doors on the rooms," he told the *Reno Gazette-Journal* in 1988. "One day I had to hock one of the girls' TV set for $50 to buy food."

Wadsworth in the 1940s featured the Nevada House Café, above left, and the Wadsworth Cash Store across the highway, dispensing Chevron gasoline. *Special Collections and University Archives Department, University of Nevada, Reno*

Finding Wadsworth

Location: 3 miles northwest of Fernley, 29 miles east of Sparks

Route: Main Street; Lincoln Highway, Virginia Street

Top: Papa's Pizzeria started out as the Wadsworth Inn c. 1870.

Above: The Union Church on another portion of the Lincoln Highway dates to 1888. *Author photos*

Top: The Mustang Ranch annex sits abandoned south of the highway between Wadsworth and Sparks.

Right: A sign prohibits those under 18 from access to the closed older portion of the Mustang Ranch. The DA burned Joe Conforte's first brothel to the ground in Wadsworth as a public nuisance, but it didn't stop Conforte from building the 51-room Mustang Ranch in 1964 for $500,000.
Author photos

Traffic on B Street in Sparks, July 1947. *Special Collections and University Archives Department, University of Nevada, Reno*

Sparks

County: Washoe
Elevation: 4,413
Established: 1904
Incorporated: 1905

1916

Population: 2,500

Accommodations: 4 hotels

Features: Garage, bank, newspaper, school, trolley

2022

Population: 108,445 (2020)

Features: Nugget Casino Resort, 3 high schools, 2 golf courses, 2 public libraries, Victorian Square, Legends shopping center

B Street, seen here in June 1939, was part of the Lincoln Highway and U.S. 40, attracting businesses like garages catering to travelers. *Special Collections and University Archives Department, University of Nevada, Reno*

Wadsworth's loss was Sparks' gain.

Sparks didn't even exist until the Southern Pacific Railroad built a railyard and maintenance depot there in 1904, transferring everything from Wadsworth.

That included its employees' homes.

The railroad dedicated five city blocks to build homes for its employees, who paid $1 a lot for them. Then, the company cut up all their homes in Wadsworth, loaded them onto rail cars in sections, and moved them for free to Sparks. It all took place on Independence Day, 1904.

The railroad went all-in on Sparks, building the largest roundhouse in the world at the time. The 40-stall facility was nearly twice the size of the one in Wadsworth

Sparks was named for Reno's governor at the time, John Sparks, after names like East Reno and Harriman (for Southern Pacific president E.H. Harriman) were rejected — the latter because Harriman didn't want the honor. The railroad would remain the economic engine that made Sparks run until the Southern Pacific transitioned from steam to diesel engines and shut down its facilities there.

The Nugget Casino had opened a few years earlier, in 1955, one of four by that name to open in a two-year period, following Yerington, Reno, and Carson City. The original Nugget on the north side of B Street featured just 50 slot machines (still a lot for the time) and a coffee shop with room for 60 customers. It expanded to the south side of B Street just three years later, transforming itself into a 36,000-square-foot behemoth with five restaurants and two bars.

Nugget mascot Last Chance Joe stands guard near the 1931 library building, which now houses the Sparks Museum. *Author photo*

The Nugget would open the first of two hotel skyscrapers in 1984 and add a second in 1996 with more than 1,400 rooms between them.

B Street was a critical artery for Sparks, funneling cars east and west through downtown along what was once the Lincoln Highway.

Interestingly, though, the original Lincoln Highway bypassed Sparks altogether, following Glendale Avenue south of town to Galletti Way, where it paralleled the Truckee River and took motorists past the Nevada Insane Asylum before deposing them on East 4th Street, which they could follow into Reno.

It was a later alignment that incorporated B Street (now Victorian Avenue) and changed the highway's route drastically.

Instead of bypassing Sparks to the south, it veered off in the opposite direction — north — along Vista Boulevard, then turned east on Prater Way for a few miles before heading south again, into the heart of town, at Pyramid Way. It then resumed its westward course along B Street before veering north again to Prater, where travelers could again continue west into Reno as Prater became 4th Street.

Passing historical downtown buildings like the depot, 1931 library building and 1905 Bank of Sparks, this route, quickly became a tourist corridor west of the city center, lined with auto courts, tourist camps, bars, cafés, and garages.

Among the first of these was the Coney Island Auto Park, which opened in 1924 on the site of a 3-acre park of the same name that had featured an artificial lake and bandstand. The Twin Cities Service Station opened that same year down the road, along with an auto camp called The Grove that provided places for travelers to pitch their tents.

The Sparks Depot. *Author photo*

AMERICA'S LONELIEST ROAD

B Street in 1939 was a wide thoroughfare lined with businesses such as McPeak Furniture, Richfield and Shell service stations, and the Electric Hotel (later the site of Sparks Theatre from 1953 to 1970, and a succession of casinos. *Special Collections and University Archives Department, University of Nevada, Reno*

The building at left in the top photo, next the two-story McPeak building in the foreground, still stands today. *Author photo*

The Sparks Theatre operated on B Street/Victorian Avenue until 1970, and then as a succession of casinos. The theater opened in 1947 with John Wayne in *Angel and the Badman*; a grand opening ad described it as the "newest and finest theatre in Nevada," with a single screen and seating for 773 patrons. *Texas2step, cinematreasures, Creative*

Finding Sparks

Location: 29 miles west of Wadsworth, directly east of Reno

Route: Glendale Avenue and Galletti Way; Vista Boulevard, Prater Way, Pyramid Way, Victorian Avenue (B Street), Rock Boulevard, 4th Street

Bank of Sparks. *Author photo*

Cabins were later added to what became the Shady Grove Motel, which was purchased by Robert Farris and renamed the Farris Motel in the late 1940s.

The City of Sparks had its own auto camp at County Road — which later became Prater — and 17th Street. Deer Park offered a gas pump, store, picnic tables, and a water pump alongside a playground, showers, and a tennis court. Mabel Smith had an auto camp two blocks down at 15th that would later become the Park Motel.

But when the city built an extension of B Street west to a new "Y" intersection with Prater, the new four-lane asphalt highway bypassed those businesses. They even sued the Sparks City Council for lost business and property values, but the new highway was a fait accompli, attracting even more tourist-oriented businesses along the corridor connecting Sparks to Reno.

Among the most visible was the Harolds Pony Express Lodge, which evolved from an earlier motel called Cremer's Auto Court founded by George Cremer in 1933 at the prime location near the Prater-B Street "Y.

The Pony Express Lodge began its existence as Cremer's Auto Court in 1933, offering "modern, insulated steam heated brick cabins" with tile baths. Nearly two decades later, it was purchased by Harolds Club owner Pappy Smith, who renovated it, added another wing, and opened a trailer court next door. You could rent a double room for $5 a night, and you could play exact duplicates of 15 slot machines found at Harolds in downtown Reno in the Pony Express lobby. Ads instructed travelers to "look for the gigantic neon sign," which was (and is) hard to miss, especially when it was lit up and the horses' legs moved at a stationary gallop and the arrow was "fired" from the Indian's bow. There was a pool, and the lodge was air-conditioned, "beautifully furnished," and equipped with "free radios throughout." Former University of Nevada track star Joe Keshmiri purchased the motel in 1989. *Author photo*

The Farris Motel and the Sandman still stand along 4th Street to greet travelers heading from Sparks into Reno. *Author photos*

Everybody's Inn Motel stands on 4th Street entering Reno from Sparks. It was open by 1944, offering "comfortable accommodations for 2 or 3 persons" and "reasonable weekly rates.

Across the street, this sign was all that remained in 2022 of the Restwell Auto Court, which was open by 1933. *Author photos*

AMERICA'S LONELIEST ROAD

CONEY ISLAND

AUTO CAMP

E. F. WHITTON, Proprietor

On the Lincoln and Victory Highways
½ Mile East of Reno — — — West Edge of Sparks
On Transcontinental and Local Buss Lines

SPACIOUS, SHADED CAMP GROUNDS

Individual Cabins — Large Garages — Service Station
General Store — Community Kitchen — Free Use of Gas
Modern Tourists Apartments

CAMP SPACE - - - - - 50c
COTTAGES - - $1.00 to $2.50

AUTHENTIC ROAD INFORMATION

This ad for the Coney Island Auto Camp advertised camping spaces for 50 cents or cottages at $1 to $2.50. *Lincoln Highway Collection of Russell Rein*

The Coney Island Bar and Restaurant was built in 1935. An article in the Nevada State Journal on January 14 announced that Laverne Sorenson, owner of the Copenhagen bar at 15th and B streets, had been granted a liquor license for a bar opposite the Coney Island Auto Camp. The bar was ultimately owned by Ralph Galletti, an Italian immigrant, and has been called "the closest thing Sparks has to a landmark." For a while, after a "re-opening" after World War II, it was known as the Coney Island Bar and Tamale Factory. *Author photos*

Above: The Reno Auto Court opened in 1928 on East 4th Street at Toano. *Lincoln Highway Collection of Russell Rein*

Left: The Hi Ho Motor Lodge could be found at the same intersection in 2022. *Author photo*

This section of Virginia Street was on the earliest version of the Lincoln Highway. By the time this photo was taken, around 1947, it was part of U.S. 395. *Photolibrarian, cinematreasures, Creative Commons 2.0*

Reno

County: Washoe
Elevation: 4,505
Established: 1868
Incorporated: 1903

1916

Population: 14,000

Accommodations: 17 hotels, camp site

Features: 8 public schools, 5 banks, 2 newspapers

2022

Population: 264,165 (2020)

Features: Reno Arch, downtown casinos; Atlantis, Peppermill, and Grand Sierra Resort casinos; University of Nevada, Reno

By the time you get to Reno, the loneliest road isn't so lonely anymore. But if you're in Reno, you aren't on U.S. 50 anymore, and the section of road that headed south to Carson City from 4th Street was only part of the Lincoln Highway until around 1920.

Before that, one highway became two at the then-future site of the Reno Arch: Virginia and Commercial Row. The Donner Route continued west, quickly jogging over to 3rd Street, while the early version of the Pioneer Route went south along Virginia, which would later be U.S. 395. The arch wasn't dedicated until 1926, when it was erected to promote the Nevada Transcontinental Highway Exposition — an event that celebrated the completion of the Lincoln and Victory highways.

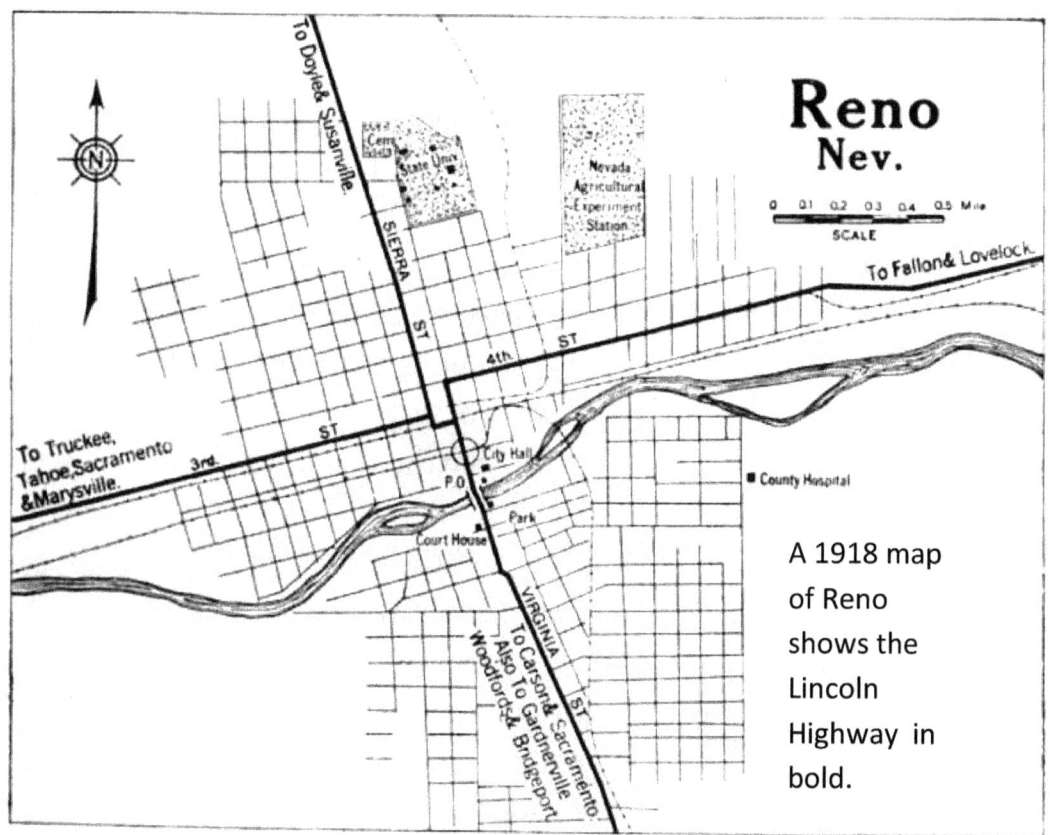

A 1918 map of Reno shows the Lincoln Highway in bold.

When the Lincoln Highway was first laid out, Reno was not only the biggest city on the road but the largest in the state with more than 10,000 residents at the 1910 census. Goldfield, now a ghost town, ranked second with 4,800, followed by Tonopah and Carson City.

> **Getting There**
>
> *Directions from the 1913 Lincoln Highway directory for the last few miles of the trip to Reno:*
>
> **0 miles:** Turn left around fence.
>
> **0.4 mile:** White House among large trees on left.
>
> **0.9 mile:** Power line on left; three wires.
>
> **0.4 mile:** Right fork; passing hospital on right; do not cross river.
>
> **1.0 mile:** Bear left into road from right with trolley on good macadam.
>
> **0.1 mile:** Water trough on right.
>
> **0.4 mile:** Bear right, leaving trolley.
>
> **0.3 mile:** Pick up trolley; now on East Fourth Street.
>
> **1.1 mile:** Turn left on North Virginia Street one block, then right and left and cross R.R. following trolley.
>
> **0.4 mile:** RENO. Riverside Hotel on right.

Las Vegas had a population of just 945 at that point.

So it made sense to route the highway through Reno, even though it meant a major detour for travelers who would have preferred to head straight to Carson City.

In 1916, *The Complete Official Guide to the Lincoln Highway* described Reno as "a fine city, and one of the most prominent in the far west," with attractions such as Steamboat Springs, and Virginia City "within easy reach of Reno."

Reno, named for Civil War Union general Jesse L. Reno, became known as "The Biggest Little City in the World," the winning slogan in a 1929 contest, submitted by a Sacramento resident. The city's iconic arch would bear that slogan for most of its history, after initially advertising the Transcontinental Highways Expo. It has taken various forms over the years, including one that featured the letters RENO in four stop-sign-shaped octagons.

Reno was originally the focal point of gambling in Nevada, with several casinos opening when they were legalized in 1931. Among the most famous and successful was Harolds Club (initially spelled Harold's Club), which opened in 1935 and promoted itself with the slogan "Harolds Club or Bust" on some 2,300 billboards across the country.

By 1953, it was the biggest business in Reno and the nation's most successful casino, grossing $15 million. A year earlier, it had averaged 10,000 customers a day. Rival Harrah's which opened in 1946, bought Harolds in 1999 and razed it. (Harrah's closed itself in 2020).

Back in the day, you could also gamble at two of downtown's biggest hotels: the Riverside and the Mapes. The six-story Riverside was built in 1927 for banking magnate George Wingfield. It houses apartments today. The Mapes, built two decades later across the street, no longer stands after being demolished on Super Bowl Sunday, January 30, 2000. Other casinos like Fitzgerald's, the Nugget, and the Horseshoe Club came and went.

Other casinos opened away from downtown, including a pair of larger developments — the Peppermill in 1985 and the Atlantis in 1996 — farther south on Virginia Street.

The Nevada-California-Oregon Railroad Depot building sits along 4th Street. Motorists traveling the old Lincoln Highway into Reno would have been greeted by the site of this building which was built in 1910. *Author photo*

Louis' Basque Corner stands a short distance from the depot. Built in 1907, it was originally the 35-room Hotel Richelieu, which served passengers disembarking trains at the station. The Lincoln Market paid tribute to the Lincoln Highway that ran past its front door, and the space later was transformed into the Lincoln Bar. After a short period as the Dude Hotel after World War II, the building became the Lincoln Hotel in the 1960s. It became Louis' Basque Corner after Louis and Lorraine Erreguible purchased the building in 1967. *Author photo*

Finding Reno

Location: Directly west of Sparks

              32 miles north of Carson City

Route: 4th Street, South Virginia Street, Commercial Row, 3rd Street

The Bonney Hotel opened across 4th Street from Louis' Basque Corner in 1931. Named for then-manager Clara Bonney, who died of pneumonia just one month later, it offered 40 rooms to travelers coming into town to gamble or to take advantage of the newly passed quickie divorce law. Businesses occupying the ground floor included a boxing gym, tire store, flower shop, and boutique. The hotel became the Bonnie Blue, Hotel Tennant, and Del Paso before E.F. Morris bought it in 1949. But like Bonney before him, he died shortly afterward, perishing in a car accident. *Author photo*

The original Reno arch has been relocated to 1 Lake Street. *Author photo*

On the highway, 1915

"Reno is a pleasant town, nobly situated on a high plateau with lofty mountains towering near. The Truckee River flows straight down from the heart of the snows through the center of town and is spanned by a handsome bridge. The substantial Riverside Hotel stands on the bank of the river near the bridge.

"Somehow, my impressions of Reno all seem to cluster around the swift river and the bridge. The library, the hotel, the Y.M.C.A., and other public buildings are all close to the river. If you walk up the river, you come to a little island in the center of the rushing stream which is a tiny Coney Island for the Reno residents during the summer."

Effie Price Gladding,
Across the Continent by the Lincoln Highway

Above: The Riverside Hotel, now an apartment building, overlooks the Virginia Street Bridge.

Right: The St. Francis Hotel was built in 1925 at a prime location, where the Lincoln Highway turned south from 4th Street onto Virginia. Hotel rooms were on the second and third floors, with a fruit market and soft drink/candy shop occupying the ground level. *Author photos*

Above: The Empire State and Chrysler buildings in New York were among the influences for the Mapes Hotel, which had a mezzanine, lobby, service floor, and Sky Room in addition to eight floors of guest rooms. Mickey Rooney, Sammy Davis Jr., and Liberace all entertained there. *Historic American Engineering Record*

Left: Harolds Club was, for a time, Reno's — and the nation's — most successful casino. *Postcard from the collection of Brian Suen*

Top: The casino strip on Virginia Street in its heyday featured gambling halls like Harrah's, the Frontier, the Nevada Club, and Harolds Club. Note that bingo was a bigger attraction than slot machines.

Above: The first Reno Arch with its original lettering and twin-flame torches.
Photos from the Lincoln Highway Collection of Russel Rein

Top: The current Reno Arch has been in place since 1986.

Above: The $100,000 Reno Arch erected in 1963 has been moved to Willits, California, where the octagonal RENO lettering has been replaced by a neon tribute to its new home. *Author photos*

Verdi

Above: These bridge rails, the first of two sets installed along the highway (the other is in Iowa) were placed on a culvert near Verdi, west of Reno in 1914. In the 1970s, they were moved to a pullout along Interstate 80.

Left: The Boomtown hotel and casino opened in 1964 as a truck stop. It now features 322 guest rooms, 39,000 square feet for gaming, restaurants, and an arcade/fun center. *Author photos*

Crystal Bay

Crystal Bay evolved as a last-chance (or first opportunity) gambling destination on Lake Tahoe's North Shore. A counterpart to Stateline in the south, it featured casinos such as the Tahoe Biltmore, which opened in 1946 and went by several other names over the years, including the Nevada Lodge and Cal-Neva Biltmore. It was said to be haunted by a ghost in a miniskirt named Mary, a former cabaret performer there. Lena Horne, Regis Philbin, and Phyllis Diller appeared there. The Tahoe Biltmore closed for good in April 2022. *Author photos*

Above: The Cal-Neva Lodge, which straddles the state line, was built in 1926 and was owned for a time in the 1960s by Frank Sinatra. He made arrangements for Marilyn Monroe to stay there on the weekend before her death. It is seen in this postcard from 1962.

Right: The Crystal Bay Club, across the street from the Tahoe Biltmore, opened in 1937 as the Ta-Neva-Ho and continues to operate as of 2022. *Author photo*

A car in the foreground, center-left, travels a road that follows the original Lincoln Highway route west of the Washoe Lake. *Author photo*

Washoe Valley

The original Lincoln Highway traveled south from Reno through the Washoe Valley, a rural expanse dominated by Washoe Lake that separates Reno from Carson City.

One of the main attractions in routing the highway this way, other than Reno, was Steamboat Springs a few miles to the south. It was at Steamboat Springs that steam escaped from a fissure in the earth with such force that none other than Mark Twain remarked upon it:

"From one spring the boiling water is ejected a foot or more by the infernal force at work below, and in the vicinity of all of them one can hear a constant rumbling and surging, somewhat resembling the noises peculiar to a steamboat in motion." That's how these springs got their name.

President Grant visited Steamboat, which became a full-fledged town in the late 19th century that included a dance hall, saloons, railroad buildings, a Grand Hotel, and a stagecoach station. In late 1900, an earthquake damaged the springs and the geyser, and a fire a few months later destroyed the hotel and other buildings in town.

Top and center: Steamboat Springs buildings in 2022. *Author photos*

Left: Steamboat Springs historic postcard. The community had a population of 23 in 1916. *Author collection*

Steamboat Springs c. 1920s or 1930s. *The Lincoln Highway Collection of Russell Rein*

Still, the hot springs remained a popular destination. *The Complete and Official Guide to the Lincoln Highway* called them "one of the wonders of nature and one of the much-spoken points on the old trail in the days of the early explorers."

A health spa was built there with buildings dating back to early 1900s.

Steamboat Springs was just a few miles north of Washoe Lake, and the road continued south from there.

Or, rather, *roads*.

Highway builders seem to have been unsure whether to plot their course along the eastern or western shore of the lake, and changed their minds about this more than once. The first alignment went to the west, through Washoe City and past historic Bowers Mansion.

Washoe City started out as a lumber camp supplying Virginia City in 1860 and became the first Washoe County seat a year later. At its peak, it boasted a population of some 6,000 residents. Unfortunately, the timber supply in the area was gradually exhausted, and millers moved up the

Sierra Nevada slopes toward Lake Tahoe, leaving Washoe City a shadow of its former self. By 1868, the newspaper had left for Reno, which had become the county seat within a couple of years. Washoe City took its case to the Nevada Supreme Court but lost.

The Washoe City Jail, which has been transformed into Washoe Zephyr Gardens, is the only building remaining from the era when Washoe City served as the Washoe County seat. *Author photo*

Washoe City was all but a ghost town by the time the Lincoln Highway came along, its courthouse having been dismantled in 1873 and its Masonic Lodge abandoned in 1888. (The most prominent business there today is the Chocolate Nugget Candy Factory.)

Still, the highway initially went that way.

It took travelers down past two historic homes, Winters and Bowers mansions along what's now called U.S. 395 Alternate, before branching west onto Franktown Road for a few miles and curling back to rejoin Alt. 395. There was actually a town at Franktown back in 1855, when the Dall Mill employed hundreds of workers, and 400 people were still living there in 1916. But as with Washoe City, it declined as woodcutters moved up the mountains and eventually disappeared entirely.

Above: The Washoe City Service Station dispensed Standard Oil products — as well as alcohol at a bar inside. *Lincoln Highway Collection of Russell Rein*

Right: A faded sign along U.S. 395 Alternate threatens motorists with up to six months in jail for speeding through Washoe City. *Author photo*

Above: The Chocolate Nugget Candy Factory has been a popular destination in modern Washoe City since 1983.

Right: A prospector welcomes customers to the Chocolate Nugget. *Author photos*

Above: Alison "Eilley" Bowers made her fortune in an unconventional way: She told fortunes for miners in Gold Hill, near Virginia City, and some of her customers paid her with a portion of their claims. Starting in 1863, she and her husband built the mansion that still stands on 395 Alternate, decking it out it with $100,000 worth of art and furnishings. Her husband died in 1868, and she was forced to sell the mansion at auction when the mining boom went bust. Today, the impressive home is the centerpiece of a regional park.

Below: Theodore Winters made a killing on the Comstock, too, so he built this mansion for himself, his wife and seven kids in 1864. The ranch eventually expanded to cover 6,000 acres, complete with a dairy and race horses.

Author photos

AMERICA'S LONELIEST ROAD

As early as 1915, a proposal was already being floated to move the highway east of the lake. The *Carson City Daily Appeal* pointed to "a low place in the hills between Carson and Washoe Valley" as a good place for the new road: "By building the road grade up the hill to the east and making the road along the east side of Washoe Valley, direct to the cut-off, it is... possible to cut down the mileage with little grade to Reno by perhaps six miles."

And a year later, the *Reno Evening Gazette* noted that "persons who are constantly using the Reno-Carson road are now using the road running on the east side of Washoe Lake, which is in much better condition than the west side" road. That road, now known as Eastlake Boulevard, became the new official Lincoln route for a time, passing through a town known as New Washoe City.

Eventually, however, modern Interstate 580 took the main route back to the west side: Today, it runs right along the water's edge, between the lake and the first Lincoln Highway (now redesignated U.S. 395 Alternate).

A section of the Lincoln Highway is preserved northeast of Washoe Lake; the road is seen coming down from the hills separating the valley from Carson City. *Author photo*

The Galena Creek Bridge is a relatively recent addition to the highway. Completed in 2012, its open-spandrel arch carries traffic on Interstate 580 on the west side of Washoe Valley, just north of Washoe Lake. At a total length of 1,725 feet, it carried an estimated 18,000 vehicles a day as of 2017. The bridge was nearly a decade in the making: Construction started in 2003. It is believed to be the world's largest concrete cathedral arch bridge. *Author photo*

Lahontan Dam, nine miles west of Fallon, was completed in 1915 — two years year after the Lincoln Highway route was set forth — as part of the Truckee-Carson Project. The Lahontan Valley wetlands are home to more than 280 species of birds. *Author photos*

The Pioneer Route

The Pioneer Route originally diverged from the Donner Route in Reno at North Virginia Street and Commercial Row, heading south through the Washoe Valley to the capital.

But advocates for the Pioneer Trail wanted a shorter path to Carson City. They sought to extend the Pioneer Route eastward, so it went from Fallon to Carson City (bypassing Reno completely) via a "Fallon Cutoff" that would provide more direct access to the capital.

A road, such as it was, already existed; it just needed to be improved and added to the highway.

So, in 1919, Goodyear Tire & Rubber Co. president Frank Seiberling donated $125,000 to the state of Nevada for work on the Lincoln Highway, with more than one-third of that ($45,000) earmarked for the Fallon Cutoff.

Lahontan Dam, seen from the air, was the nation's largest earth and gravel fill dam at the time of its completion. *U.S. Bureau of Reclamation*

The branch originally left the Donner Route at Lahontan Dam, shaving 31 miles off the route that had detoured north to Reno before finally reaching Carson. By 1921, the route was established from west of Fallon to the state capital, passing through communities such as Dayton along the way.

It entered Carson City along William Street (not to be confused with Williams Street in Fallon) then jogged south along Carson Street before heading west again into the Sierra Nevada. The original route climbed into the mountains via Kings Canyon Road, before rejoining the current U.S. 50 route near Spooner Summit.

The Kings Canyon route had been cleared as early as 1852 as an alternative path through the mountains via Eagle Valley. It served as a major stage wagon and freight toll road from 1863 to 1875.

Later, U.S. 50 heading west from Carson City was rerouted along Old Clear Creek Road, farther to the south, and this was, in turn, replaced by a new highway around 1960.

Silver Springs

The sign for the Silver Springs Nugget is almost as big as the casino, which stands at the junction of U.S. 50 and U.S. 95 Alternate. The traffic-circle junction serves as a gateway to historical sites such as Fort Churchill and Buckland Station.

Detour: Fort Churchill

Fort Churchill, a few miles south of U.S. 50 on U.S. 95 Alternate, was built in 1860 as an Army outpost to protect settlers in the region and Pony Express riders from Native American raids. The adobe ruins of the fort, abandoned in 1869 after it was deemed too costly to operate, remain. Above is what's left of the officers' quarters. *Author photos*

Top: Fort Churchill is seen, slightly better preserved, in this 1958 photo. *National Survey of Historic Sites and Buildings*

Above: Pioneers traveling the Overland Trail had been stopping at Samuel Buckland's ranch for a decade by the time he built this two-story stagecoach station from wood and other materials he salvaged from the newly abandoned Army post at Fort Churchill, just two miles down the road. *Author photo*

Stagecoach

The Oasis Restaurant with its distinctive cactus (possibly clever camouflage for a pump house) sits abandoned off the U.S. 50 frontage road in Stagecoach. The unincorporated community was likely for its location at the former Desert Well Overland Trail stagecoach station. *Author photos*

> Apparently, there isn't much real estate for sale in Stagecoach these days.
> *Author photo*

Sutro

Sutro was named for Adolph Sutro, a Prussian immigrant who served as mayor of San Francisco from 1895 to 1897. But he was perhaps more famous for building the Sutro Tunnel east of Dayton three decades earlier. A

tobacco salesman, he made a fortune at Virginia City off the Comstock Lode.

Sutro, left, arrived in Virginia City in 1860, a couple of years before Mark Twain started working at the *Territorial Enterprise* newspaper. Five years later, he devised a scheme to construct a tunnel that would reduce the threat of flooding by draining water out of the shafts.

He didn't have the financing he needed for construction, however, until 1869, after a fire erupted in the Yellow Jacket mine at nearby Gold Hill, killing at least 35 workers in Nevada's worst-ever mining disaster. Miners, fearful of another tragic accident, swung their support behind the project, which ultimately cost $3.5 million and stretched nearly four miles when it was completed in 1878.

A town even grew up around the tunnel's mouth.

By that time, however, the Comstock was past its peak production, so the tunnel itself never turned a profit.

Top: The town of Sutro in 1874, four years before the tunnel was completed. *Crispy1234, Creative Commons 4.0*

Above: The entrance to the Sutro Tunnel. *Historic American Buildings Survey*

Dayton

County: Lyon *(county seat, 1861-1911)*
Elevation: 4,296
Established: 1851
Unincorporated

1916
    Population: 517
    Accommodations: Hotels
    Features: High school, Odeon Hall, mill, saloons

2022
    Population: 15,153 (2020)
    Features: Casinos, retail stores, restaurants, service stations

A drive through Dayton's historical district reveals a gold rush town with much of its heritage intact. Along with Genoa, which makes the same assertion, Dayton can lay claim to being the first settlement in Nevada. Abner Blackburn discovered gold nearby in 1849 on his way to California, and a mining settlement called Gold Cañon Flat was thriving there by the following year.

In 1857, Chinese miners began making their way to the area from California, which had adopted a mining tax on Chinese workers. By 1860, they were the dominant presence in the area — so much so that the U.S. Census Bureau grouped the area's 78 residents there together as "Chinatown."

The town went through a variety of other names, such as Ponderer's Rest and McMartin Station, before settling on Dayton ("Day Town") in honor of surveyor John Day, who laid out the townsite.

By the time the Lincoln Highway ran through town in the 1920s, Dayton was already almost three-quarters of a century old and had survived fires that had all but destroyed the town in 1866 and again in 1870.

This building behind a gas station at 65 Silver Street, just off U.S. 50, was operating as a coffeehouse in 2022. But it started off as "China Mary's House." Ty Kim, aka China Mary, ran a market there. The structure is the only one remaining in Dayton from its initial era as Chinatown. *Author photos*

In 1923, the *Automobile Blue Book* described the highway between Fallon and Silver Springs as "natural prairie road... with some rough stretches around Lahontan Lake." But most of the distance between the "prominent fork" at Silver Springs and the capital was "graded gravelly dirt" through "open, rolling prairie country" and "an irrigated valley" nearer Carson.

That included Dayton, where the road ran briefly north and south.

It entered town from the north on Pike Street, then jogged west on Main to River Street, which it followed south to the edge of town before veering westward again on its primary trajectory.

The road ran through the heart of what's now Dayton's historic district, where travelers could stop for the night at one of the downtown hotels and have a drink at one of several saloons in the area. Not far away was the 1918 high school, which had been built on the site of Dayton's courthouse. The seat of government burned in 1909, paving the way for Yerington to claim the Lyon County seat two years later.

The Lincoln Highway north of Dayton is blocked off to vehicle traffic, but you can still walk on this segment of gravel and cracked concrete.
Author photo

The 1918 Dayton High School on Pike Street, top, replaced the 1864 County Courthouse, above, that burned in 1909.

The Lincoln Highway in Dayton ran along Pike Street, past the 1875 firehouse, below, and the Odeon Hall, at right above, to the Union Hotel at Main Street. The firehouse also became home to the jail in 1909, when cells purchased by mail order in the 1860s were relocated there. *Author photos*

Top: The Odeon was built on the site of an Oddfellows hall dating to 1862. The paddleball scene from Marilyn Monroe's 1960 film *The Misfits* was filmed there. One of the oldest theaters and saloons in Nevada, it boasted a grand ballroom upstairs.

Right: The Union Hotel opened around the same time, in 1870. *Author photos*

Top: The stone building at Pike and Main was originally home to M. Meyer and Co., a grocer, but later housed a hardware store and (briefly before the turn of the century) the post office. It later became Braun & Loftus General Merchandise and the Old Corner Bar. The sign out front is from a burned-down restaurant in Carson City, Adele's.

Above: This 1885 saloon was moved to its current Main Street location in 1904 as the Europa. Once a boarding house, it was the site of a duel in which a mustached man, who reportedly haunts the building, was killed. *Author photos*

Top: Built in the late 1860s, this sturdy Main Street structure served as home to Bluestone Manufacturing. The mural on its side pays tribute to Tahoe Beer, which was brewed in Carson City on another section of the Lincoln Highway, King Street.

Above: The Fox Hotel on Main was the Occidental from 1889 to 1907. *Author photos*

The Rock Point Mill alongside U.S. 50 was built for $200,000 in 1861 as Nevada's first large quartz mill. It burned in 1882 and again in 1909 but was rebuilt both times before finally being dismantled and moved to Silver City in 1920. Water from Rock Point Dam was brought in to power it on a 2,000-foot wooden flume. *Author photos*

Detour: Silver City

Historic buildings in Silver City include the firehose, top, and Donovan Mill, right. The town is a little more than three miles north of U.S. 50 via Nevada Routes 341 and 342. Two brothers found silver there in 1856 but died before they could get it assayed. Had they done so, they would have discovered the Comstock Lode. *Author photos*

Top: Hardwicke House, built in 1862, was once an icehouse and also served as a bed and breakfast.
Sharon Stora

Above: A building in Silver City advertises Tahoe Beer.
Author photo

Detour: Gold Hill

Gold Hill is about 5½ miles north of U.S. 50 on Nevada Route 342 and 341. Less well known than its neighbor to the north, Virginia City, the Comstock boomtown was nonetheless a force to be reckoned with. It was at its peak in the late 1870s, when this photo was taken. The population of 638 in 1860 had swollen to 4,311 a decade later and hit 4,531 in 1880. *Carleton Watkins, Western Nevada Historic Photo Collection*

Gold Hill Depot. *Author photo*

Above: Gold Hill Miners' Union building. *National Park Service*

Below: The Gold Hill Bank did business in this building from the time it opened in 1862 until 1873, then the Bank of California operated there until 1879. *Author photo*

Above: The Gold Hill Hotel, the front stone portion of which was built around 1859, is the oldest in Nevada. It's said to be haunted by the ghost of a prostitute named Rosie and a former owner named William. Guests claim to have smelled her perfume in Room 4 and his cigar smoke in Room 5.

Right: The Yellow Jacket Mine is next to the hotel's miner's cabin, where guests say they've encountered the ghost of a miner killed in the Yellow Jacket fire that killed 35 on April 7, 1869. *Author photo*

Detour: Virginia City

Virginia City was a thriving metropolis in 1875 at the epicenter of the Comstock Lode, which yielded an unprecedented gold and silver boom. An estimated 25,000 people lived there when this photo was taken, far more than in any other Nevada city. (Nearby Gold Hill ranked second.) *Carleton Watkins*

Virginia City in 1866. *Library of Congress*

The International Hotel opened in 1877 as the tallest building in Nevada with 160 rooms in six stories. Across the street from Piper's Opera House, it was the successor to the first International Hotel at Union between B and C streets, which had been built in 1860 and gone up in flames in 1875. First-class rooms with gas lighting cost $2.50 a night or $55 a month in the new "Palatial Palace." The hotel finally went electric with the rest of the town in 1900. Unfortunately, a kitchen fire brought the grand hotel down in 1914, but only about a dozen people were staying there at the time, and no lives were lost. *Library of Congress*

Top: This street scene from 1938 shows an ad for Coca-Cola outside the original Bucket of Blood Saloon.

Above: The *Territorial Enterprise* declared the new Fourth Ward School "the finest structure of its kind in Nevada" when it opened in 1876. The four-story school at the south end of C Street was built to house 1,000 students. But fewer than 200 remained by the 1930s, and the school closed in 1936, a year before this photo was taken. The ghost of a teacher named Suzette is said to haunt the school. *Library of Congress*

The Washoe Club, an exclusive social organization catering to the wealthy and elite in Virginia City. Its guest register included names such as Ulysses S. Grant; Virginia & Truckee Railroad co-owner Darius Odgen Mills (president of the Bank of California and for a time the richest man in that state); famed Shakespearean actor Edwin Booth (inset; the older brother of president Lincoln's assassin, John Wilkes Booth); and humorist-author Artemus Ward. The three-story building was built in 1862, and the social club, organized in the 1860s, moved there in 1875 after its original location burned. *Author photos*

Originally, the building that later hosted the Washoe Club housed retail spaces, offices, and miners' quarters on the top floor. When the Washoe Club began meeting there, it included a billiard room, wine room, parlor decorated with marble and bronze statuettes, and a poker room upstairs still said to house the original high-stakes table, pictured below. The world's longest freestanding spiral staircase was installed (photo on previous page), and the building also had a room where, according to one account, bodies were piled in winter while morticians waited for the ground to thaw out. The practice is said to have continued from 1870 until 1922, and one particularly bad winter (1874), 77 bodies were reportedly piled up there in burlap sacks. Or is this just a tall tale? Imagine the stench! Not surprisingly, the Washoe is said to be haunted by several ghosts. Most prominent among them is a prostitute named Leana, aka the "Lady in Blue," who reportedly haunts the spiral staircase wearing a blue Victorian-style dress. The ghost of a young girl who was run over by a horse-drawn carriage in the street out front way back in 1864 is also said to be present. *Author photos*

Right: Entrance to an underground tunnel temporarily exposed by the demolition of a building on C Street.

Below: Faded lettering for the Crystal Bar and a hardware store next door

According to a 2003 article in the *Los Angeles Times*, between 350 and 750 miles of tunnels lie beneath Virginia City's streets, from mining tunnels to discrete passageways through which men would exit places like the Washoe Club and stroll down to the red-light district for an illicit rendezvous. *Author photos*

Top: The Union Brewery dates to 1865, but this building was erected after an earlier structure burned in the Great Fire of 1875. Faded ads still can be seen on the outside walls.

Above: The Tahoe House Hotel dates to 1859. *Author photos*

Top: The Bonanza Saloon building dates to 1870.

Above: The *Territorial Enterprise* moved to Virginia City from Carson City in 1860 and once employed a reporter named Samuel Clemens. *Author photos*

Right: The Storey County Courthouse sits on the site of the first courthouse, which was burned in the Great Fire of 1875. *Author photos*

Above: Piper's Opera House opened in 1862 as Tom Maguire's D Street Theatre. John Piper purchased it in 1868, but it burned down twice and he ultimately rebuilt it on B Street, its present location. Maude Adams, Lily Langtry, Houdini, Enrico Caruso, and Mark Twain all appeared at Piper's. Other events included bear wrestling, political debates, roller skating, basketball, movies, and dances.

Mound House, just over the county line from Carson City, is the only place in Lyon County where brothels are legal. The limit is four. The most famous is the Moonlite BunnyRanch, top, north of U.S. 50, which was founded as the Moonlight Ranch in 1955 and purchased by Dennis Hof in 1992. The Red Light Adult Cabaret, above, is across the highway in a "red light district" south of U.S. 50. *Author photos*

Top: Eastbound U.S. 50 heading out of Carson City under the Virginia & Truckee Railroad bridge. The railroad was incorporated in 1868 to connect Carson City and, later, Reno with the Comstock mines.

Above: Westbound U.S. 50 approaching Carson City. *Author photos*

Top: Gold Dust West Casino Hotel opened on U.S. 50 in the 1990s as Piñon Plaza. It was strategically situated at the future site of an interchange with planned Interstate 580 (the 395 bypass). *Author photo*

Above: Wild horses gather just east of Carson City off U.S. 50. *Sharon Stora*

The former Lucky Spur Casino, left, is now the Union Brewery on U.S. 395 in Carson City. *Author photo*

U.S. 395 entering Carson City from the north.
Author photo

The loneliest Road in America

Carson City to Tahoe

Whether you arrived in Carson City from the north via Reno, or from the east from Fallon, there was little doubt you had arrived at an important destination. While not as large as Reno, Carson City was the seat of government for Nevada, first as a territory in 1861 and then when it attained statehood in 1864.

The original Lincoln Highway wound its way south into Carson from the Washoe Valley onto Carson Street, continuing down past the U.S. Mint building and the ornate 1891 federal building to West King Street, opposite the state Capitol Building. King is blocked off opposite the Capitol these days, but when the Lincoln Highway was laid out, it was possible to turn west onto King, motor on past the 1864 Carson Brewing Company Building, and head up into the Sierra Nevada via the road that became known as Kings Canyon.

The dirt and gravel route, which still exists, would deposit you on the other side near Spooner Summit, whence it would take you down to Lake Tahoe.

Later, after the Fallon Cutoff became part of the Lincoln Highway, it was extended farther south on Carson Street, past the St. Charles Hotel (built in 1862 but called the Golden West by 1910 and the Travelers Hotel starting in 1928), and the 1899 Bank Saloon south of town to Old Clear Creek Canyon. There, this newer Lincoln route would take you west, roughly paralleling the modern highway's path, until it joined the current route just east of Spooner Summit.

Then it was on to Glenbrook, Zephyr Cove, and Stateline along Tahoe's eastern short, before the Pioneer Route swept south and west again into California. Passing through communities like Pollock Pines, Placerville, and Folsom, mostly along current U.S. 50, it would be reunited with the Donner Route in Sacramento.

Replica Lincoln Highway marker outside the 1863 Carson City Mint building, now part of the Nevada State Museum. *Author photo*

Carson City

County: Carson City *(territorial capital 1861; state capital 1864; county seat of Ormsby County until 1969)*
Elevation: 4,802
Established: 1858
Incorporated: 1875

1916
    Population: 3,000
    Accommodations: 4 hotels
    Features: 4 garages, 1 bank, 85 general businesses, 3 newspapers, state penitentiary, Stewart Indian School, State Capitol, Mint

2022
    Population: 58,639 (2020)
    Features: State Capitol, airport, several casinos, interstate freeway, Nevada State Museum, Railroad Museum, parks, public schools

Carson City was full of history before the Lincoln Highway came through. Named for Kit Carson, the pioneer who served as a scout on John C. Frémont's expedition westward in 1843. Frémont named the Carson River in his honor, and the city's name ultimately sprang from that.

But Carson City was still more than a decade from becoming reality.

Fifteen years after Frémont and Carson visited the area, businessman Abe Curry and two attorneys from Utah — John Musser and Frank Proctor — found themselves in Genoa. Curry intended to start a mercantile there, but his offer of $1,000 for a lot was rejected, so they set their sights on the Eagle Valley, about 13 miles to the north, instead.

They arrived there in 1858, and Genoa Mayor William Ormsby followed. He built a two-story hotel there in the fledgling city that Proctor named "Carson." The county, meanwhile, was named Ormsby.

Warm Springs Hotel was the site of the Nevada Territorial Legislature's first meeting, on October 1, 1861. *Public domain*

Curry built a hotel of his own out by Warm Springs in 1861, then sold some of the nearby land to the state for $80,000. It became the site of Nevada State Prison. Another early visitor to Carson City was Samuel Clemens, whose older brother Orion served as the first secretary of Nevada Territory and built a home there in 1862. The younger Clemens worked as a reporter for the *Territorial Enterprise* in Virginia City but filed many of his reports from Carson City, including a letter which he signed for the first time using his soon-to-be-famous pen name, Mark Twain.

Another famous 19th century Carson City resident was Washington Gale Ferris, who lived at Third and Division streets in his youth. Later, as an adult, he created the first Ferris Wheel for the 1893 World's Columbian Exhibition in Chicago. Designed to rival the Eiffel Tower in scope and grandeur, it was a gigantic contraption featuring 36 cars with a capacity of 60 people each.

In 1897, middleweight champ Bob Fitzsimmons came to town to challenge "Gentleman" Jim Corbett for his heavyweight title before 4,000 fans in Carson City. Corbett knocked Fitzsimmons down in the sixth round, but the smaller man recovered to KO the champ in the 14th with a shot to the solar plexus.

Carson City was a railroad town early on, with the Virginia & Truckee Railroad connecting it to Virginia City during the Comstock boom. (Curry, who also built the U.S. Mint on Carson Street, where his ghost allegedly resides, constructed the machine and car shops at the city's rail yard.)

But as time passed and the automobile grew more prominent, it became a key stop on the highway, as well.

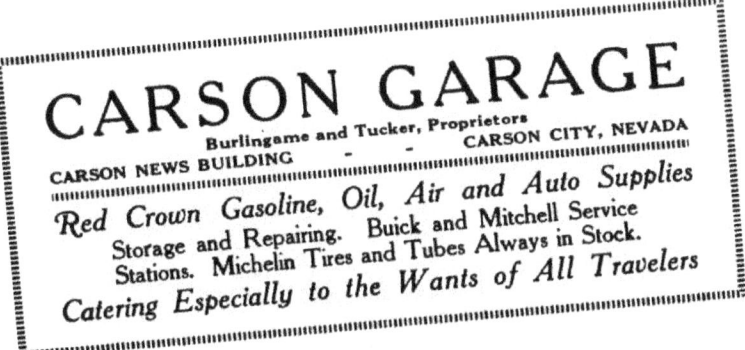

Travelers could have their cars checked at Raycraft's Garage on North Carson Street, where they could buy gas and lubricating oils, as well as at the V&T Railroad shops. James Raycraft also owned a hotel with his brother Joseph at Carson and Musser streets, so motorists had a place to stop for the night.

By 1916, the Carson Garage was operating out of the Carson News Building, dispensing Red Crown Gasoline and Michelin Tires. It placed an ad in the *Complete Official Guide to the Lincoln Highway* alerting drivers it was open for business.

On the highway, 1924

"[Carson City is] beautifully laid out and claims the distinction of having more shade and fruit trees than any other city in the state."

Complete Official Road Guide to the Lincoln Highway, 1924

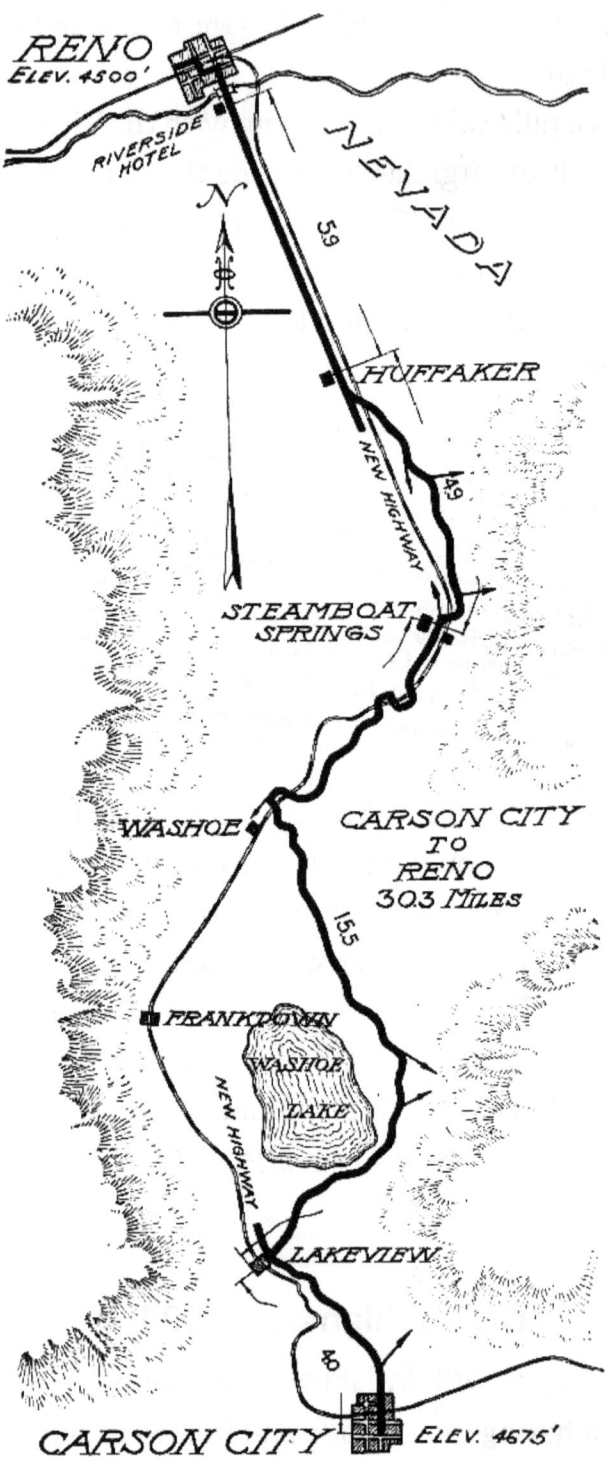

The road between Carson City and Reno before the advent of the Lincoln Highway is shown in this 1912 map from the *California State Automobile Association Tour Book*.

U.S. 395 at the north end of Carson continued to be a well-traveled gateway to the capital long after it ceased to be part of the Lincoln Highway, with travelers stopping at motels such as the Frontier, with its distinctive neon sign. The Frontier was already operating, as Dorothy's Auto Court, in the 1930s. *Author photos*

Entering town from the east on U.S. 50, you could stay at the Desert Air Motel 1½ miles east of the city "for the rest of your life," or Sam Preston's Hi-Way 50 Motel, seen here in 2022, which offered "shady parking" and one- and two-room units with "air foam mattresses for comfort." It has since been transformed into a strip mall, with no shady parking in evidence.

Farther south on Carson Street, which was cosigned as U.S. 395 and U.S. 50 between William Street and Old Clear Creek Canyon, travelers could choose from overnight stays at places like the Desert Hills Motel, which offered "Carson City's newest, all-modern deluxe units" with free TV and wall-to-wall carpets in 1959, or the historic St. Charles, which was known by a variety of names over the years, including the Hotel Page after World War II and the Pony Express starting in 1953. *Author collection, photo*

The Gateway Motel, not pictured, and the Mill House Motel were two other options for travelers on U.S. 50/395. The Gateway, which advertised itself as the "gateway to the 1960 Olympics," offered 27 units with individual heat and tubs or showers. The Mill House, a mile south of town, provided a heated pool and individually controlled AC. Unlike the other two, it's still in business, although without its once-imposing giant sign. *Author collection, author photo*

Finding Carson City

Location: 63 miles west of Fallon
    32 miles south of Reno,
    16 miles east of Glenbrook (west shore Lake Tahoe)
The route: Portions of Carson, King, William streets; Kings Canyon Road; Old Clear Creek Canyon

The State Capitol west front, across Carson Street, in 1972. *Historic American Buildings Survey, Library of Congress*

Looking east on King Street toward the State Capitol. *Author photo*

George W. Kitzmeyer built the Kitzmeyer Furniture Factory in 1873 at Carson and Telegraph streets. It's the most intact example of late-19th century Italianate commercial architecture in Carson City. *Author photos*

The Carson Theatre opened in 1933 at the northeast corner of Carson and Robinson streets. Today, the building houses a coin dealer.

The first alignment of the Lincoln Highway went past the Carson Brewery Co. building on King Street, which was built in 1864 and where Tahoe Beer was brewed starting in 1913.

Customers gather at the bar in the Carson Brewery in 1940. The building later served as a newspaper office and an arts center.
Arthur Rothstein, Library of Congress

Top: U.S. 50 joins U.S. 395 at William and Carson streets.

Above: The Carson Nugget Casino opened in 1954 at Carson and Robinson.
Author photos

Two views of the 1891 federal building, which housed the post office, weather bureau, land office, and U.S. District Court, on Carson Street, with Cactus Jack's Casino in the foreground below. The former Senator Club became Cactus Jack's in 1971 when it was purchased by Peter "Cactus Pete" Piersanti. *Author photos*

Right: A sign marks Kings Canyon Road west of Carson City as the Pioneer Route of the Lincoln Highway.

Below: The view of Carson City, looking east from the end of the paved portion of Kings Canyon Road. *Author photos*

Two views of the old Lincoln Highway's gravel route over Kings Canyon Road west of Carson City." *Author photos*

Right: Clear Creek picnic area, 1939. *Nevada Department of Transportation*

Below: Old Clear Creek Canyon Road west of Carson City. *Author photo*

Top: Old Clear Creek Canyon Road, former U.S. 50, west of Carson City. *Author photo*

Above: Opening ceremony for the modern U.S. 50 through Clear Creek Canyon in 1957.

Right: Abandoned section of old U.S. 50 in Clear Creek Canyon, 1960. *Nevada Department of Transportation*

Glenbrook

The first version of the Lincoln Highway through Kings Canyon exits onto the modern highway near the Spooner Summit trailhead, west of Lake Tahoe, where it joined the Clear Creek Toll Road. *Author photo*

The highway greets Lake Tahoe at Glenbrook on the eastern shore, founded in 1860. The Glenbrook Inn, seen here in 1915, opened in 1907 and offered "those who want genuine summer outing… excellent hotel accommodations or the cottage life if desired." *George Wharton James*

Cave Rock

Glenbrook, population 250, was the first place west of Carson City where you could find gas, a meal, and a room for the night in 1916. Cave Rock was next on the Complete and Official Guide's itinerary, seven miles away, but it was "only a landmark." A single-lane hanging bridge and rock wall built in 1863 carried the Lincoln Highway past it. The first of two tunnels bored through the cliff was completed in 1931, with the second being added in 1957 to create a four-lane road. *Author photos*

Zephyr Cove

Above: A boat skims the water on Lake Tahoe from a U.S. 50 overlook.

Below: A steamboat is docked at Zephyr Cove. *Author photos*

Above: A historic marker shows a short, abandoned section of the Lincoln Highway as a dirt road just north of the Zephyr Cove Lodge parking lot and west of modern U.S. 50. The sign notes that the highway generally followed the route of the 1863 Lake Bigler Toll Road in Tahoe.

Right: A portion of the highway just south of the above photo remains as this paved parking road. *Author photos*

Above: Zephyr Cove on Lake Tahoe's western shore got its name in 1862 from the Washoe Zephyr, a summer late-afternoon wind in the area. A post office opened there in 1930. A newspaper account in 1940 referred to "the new lodge built by Mr. and Mrs. C. Wylie" as including "20 hotel rooms, a modern coffee shop and game room." The lodge was finished in knotty pine and maple, with early American furniture.

Right: The Pine Cone Resort on the opposite side of U.S. 50 has been open since 1955. The neon sign advertises a heated swimming pool, and a 1960s-era postcard touted "comfortable, lake view housekeeping units with fireplaces" along with a view of Lake Tallac. *Author photos*

Stateline

Casinos line U.S. 50 on the Nevada side of the California state line. William Harrah set up shop at Tahoe in 1955, when he bought George's Gateway Club, which is now Harveys (founded by Harvey Gross in 1944). The Harveys tower opened in 1963. Bally's, right, began as the Park Tahoe in 1978, was Caesars Tahoe from 1979 to 2006, and MontBleu from then until 2021. *Author photos*

The Hard Rock Casino has undergone several incarnations. It started out as the Sahara Tahoe in 1965. (Elvis performed there from 1971 to '76.) It became the High Sierra in 1983, the Horizon Lake Tahoe in 1990, and finally the Hard Rock in 2014. *Author photo*

Right: The Stateline Country Club Café and Market in 1930.

Harveys, top, operated the Lakeside Inn from 1972 to 1985. It opened as Caesars Inn in 1969 with 100 slot machines and five table games, later expanding to about 130 rooms. It closed permanently in 2020 in response to the COVID pandemic. *Author photo*

Highway Timeline
Selected highlights

1860 — Pony Express established
1861 — Pony Express mail service discontinued
        Fort Churchill completed
1862 — Austin designated Lander County seat
1863 — International Hotel moved from Virginia City to Austin
1864 — Carson City named capital of Nevada
        Eureka named county seat of newly formed Eureka County
1869 — Fort Churchill abandoned
1878 — Sutro Tunnel opens
1887 — White Pine County seat moved from Hamilton to Ely
1897 — Stokes Castle built in Austin
1898 — Post office established at Fallon
1903 — Churchill County seat moved from Stillwater to Fallon
1904 — Post office established at Hazen
1907 — Northern Hotel opens in Ely
        McGill Drugstore opens
        Glenbrook Inn opens
1908 — Overland Hotel opens in Fallon on future Lincoln Highway

1908 — White Pine County Courthouse opens in Ely

1909 — Lyon County Courthouse burns in Dayton

1910 — Number of vehicles registered in Nevada: 450 cars, 10 trucks

1911 — Nevada appropriates $20,000 for Ormsby County road work

1912 — Nevada legislature establishes state highway from Ely through Eureka, Austin, Fallon, Reno, and Carson City to California (highway never completed for lack of funds)

        Indianapolis Motor Speedway owner Carl Fisher announces plan for a "Coast-to-Coast Rock Highway."

1913 — Original Lincoln Highway Route established

        Lincoln Highway enters Nevada four miles west of Ibapah, Utah

        Lincoln Highway Route, Road Conditions and Directions published

1914 — Just 262 of Nevada's 12,182 miles of roadway are surfaced with oil and gravel

        Iconic Lincoln Highway bridge railings placed on now-demolished concrete culvert bridge in Verdi

1915 — *Across the Continent By the Lincoln Highway* published

        Donner branch of Lincoln Highway rerouted through Sparks

        Lahontan Dam completed

        Number of cars and trucks registered in Nevada tops 2,000

1916 — Plans for Stillwater Cutoff established

        Complete Official Guide to the Lincoln Highway published

        Water distribution from Lahontan Dam begins

        Lincoln Highway signed from Ely to California state line by California State Automobile Association

1918 — Branch road from Lahontan Dam to Carson City described as being on the Lincoln Highway

1919 — General Motors contributes $100,000 to the Lincoln Highway Association for improvements to the road, including at Fallon Sink

        LHA donates $45,000 for improvements to 17.3 miles of road between Grimes Ranch and Sand Springs

1920 — New gravel route over Austin Summit has a maximum 6 percent grade compared with the previous route's 12 percent

Ten-mile segment of road between Salt Wells and Sand Springs completed, replacing the Stillwater Cutoff

Rex Theatre opens in Fallon

1921 — Route through Sparks, Reno cosigned with Victory Highway

Fallon Cutoff opens to regular travel

Goodyear Cutoff project in Utah abandoned

Number of cars registered in Nevada hits 10,000

Under the Federal Aid Highway Act of 1921, Nevada receives 87 percent of its funding for highway building from the federal government

1922 — New route established between Eureka and Hay Ranch at a cost of $95,000

Lincoln Highway Association donates $107,500 for four segments of road in Eureka and Churchill counties, but not all the money is used

1923 — Lincoln Highway shifts its alignment from Ibapah, Utah, north through West Wendover

Road from Carson City to Lake Tahoe moved from Kings Canyon to Old Clear Creek Road

1924 — Nevada Department of Highways and White Pine County complete a new alignment from west of Illipah to Pancake Summit, 250 feet lower in elevation than its predecessor

1925 — Realignment over Carroll Summit completed

Texaco station opens near Carroll Summit

1926 — U.S. adopts federal highway system, replacing auto trails

Bill Smith opens State Line Service station at West Wendover

Reno Arch erected to honor completion of Lincoln and Victory highways

1928 — Section of highway between Wendover and McGill approved

More than 25,000 cars registered in Nevada for the first time

1929 — Hotel Nevada opens in Ely
1930 — Lincoln Highway Days Festival in Ely
1931 — State Line Service adds hotel, casino in West Wendover
　　　　Capitol Club, Copper Club, Miners Club casinos open in Ely
　　　　Owl Club, Sagebrush Club casinos open in Fallon
　　　　First Cave Rock tunnel bored at Lake Tahoe
1934 — U.S. 40 in Sparks rerouted from Prater Way to new B Street extension (Victorian Avenue) between 15th Street and newly created Y junction
1937 — By this time, most of Lincoln Highway through Nevada has been redesignated as U.S. 50
1942 — NAS Fallon opens
1944 — Harvey's Wagon Wheel opens at Stateline, Tahoe
　　　　Hazen store opens
1949 — Nevada automobile registrations surpass 50,000
1952 — "Wendover Will" begins greeting travelers at the Utah-Nevada state line
1954 — Carson Nugget casino opens
1956 — Nevada car registrations top 100,000 for the first time
1957 — New highway opens through Clear Creek Canyon, west of Carson City
1963 — New Reno Arch erected for $100,000
1966 — More than 300,000 cars now registered in Nevada
1967 — U.S. 50 Carroll Summit section moved to New Pass
1972 — Number of trucks registered in Nevada surpasses 100,000
1979 — Battle Mountain replaces Austin as Lander County seat
1981 — Nevada car registrations top 500,000
1986 — Great Basin National Park established
　　　　Current Reno Arch erected
1987 — Frenchman Station buildings demolished
2012 — Galena Creek Bridge opens in Washoe Valley

Sources

"40 Mile Desert," californiatrailcenter.org.
"Austin Historic District," National Register of Historic Places Inventory – Nomination Form, npgallery.nps.gov.
"Automobile Notes," Reno Evening Gazette, p. 2, Aug. 26, 1916.
Barber, Alicia. "Louis' Basque Corner," renohistorical.org.
Barber, Alicia. "Morris Motel," renohistorical.org.
Barber, Alicia. "Piazzo Building," renohistorical.org.
Barber, Alicia. "Pony Express Lodge," renohistorical.org.
"Before Ely, there was Lane City," Nevada Appeal, Aug. 8, 2013.
"A Brief History," mcgillnevada.com.
"Buckland Station," travelnevada.com.
"Carroll Summit Station," forgottennevada.org.
"Casino Overview," Stockman's Casino, stocmanscasino.com.
"The Complete Official Road Guide of the Lincoln Highway," Lincoln Highway Association, 1916.
Coney Island Bar and Tamale Factory ad, Nevada State Journal, p. 14, April 11, 1947.
"Coney Island Resort (site)," renohistorical.org.
"Conforte to retire," Reno Gazette-Journal, p. 14, July 30, 1988.
Corona, Marcella. "Haunted Virginia: 11 eerie places to see this Halloween," rgj.com, Oct. 12, 2021.
"Cut-off Road is Proposed Between Reno and Carson," Carson City Daily Appeal, p. 1, Aug. 28, 1915.
Dowd, Katie. "Developer buys 75-year-old Tahoe Biltmore hotel," sfgate.com, Oct. 17, 2021.
"Duke's Casino Building Down the Years," Sparks Today, Reno Gazette-Journal, p. 3, Aug. 9, 2005.
Durski, Brad F. "Nevada's Galena Creek Bridge," Aspire, Winter 2010.
"Ely Hotel Burns," Reno Evening Gazette, p. 1, May 18, 1964.
"Ely Theatre," Cinematreasures.org.
Estrada, Garrett. "Ghost Stories," elynews.com, Oct. 30, 2015.
"Eureka: Friendly town with a haunted history," abc4.com, March 22, 2019.

"Eureka Self-Guiding Tour," rainesmarket.com.
Everybody's Inn classified ad, Reno Evening Gazette, p. 11, April 24, 1944.
"Fallon Mud Flats Terrors Are No More," Reno Evening Gazette, p. 10, June 10, 1922.
"Fallon Theatre," cinematreasures.org.
"Farris Motel," renohistorical.org.
"Fernley," nvexpeditions.com.
"Fernley Swales cleanup," canvocta.org.
"Forty Mile Desert," nv-landmarks.com.
"Frenchman's Station aka Bermond," onlinenevada.org.
"Galena Creek Bridge," bridgehunter.com.
"Ghost Adventures: Beneath the Bonanza," travelchannel.com.
"Glenbrook Inn and Ranch," San Francisco Examiner, p. 7, May 16, 1907.
"The Goodyear Conflict," ccmuseum.omeka.net.
Goulding, Effie Price. "Across the Continent By the Lincoln Highway," Brentano's, New York, 1915.
"Gray Reid's – Nevada's Fine Store," bigmallrat.blogspot.com, July 6, 2011.
Haas, Greg. "Tribute to Constitution spelled out in rocks on US 50 in Nevada," 8newsnow.com, Sept. 21, 2020.
"Hamilton," ghosttowns.com.
"Hamilton (White Pine County)," forgottennevada.org.
Harmon, Mella. "Mapes Hotel (site)," renohistorical.org.
"Harold's Club," oldreno.net (web archive).
Harolds Pony Express ad, Reno Evening Gazette, p. 9, Aug. 22, 1956.
"Hickison Burro Herd," travelnevada.com.
"Haunted Places in Fallon, Nevada," hauntedplaces.org.
"Hickison Summit," onlinenevada.org.
"Hickison Summit (aka Hickerson Summit in the 1930's)," cmdrmark.com.
"Highway Department Busy," Yerington Times, p. 1, July 26, 1919.
"Historic Austin Hotel Is Sold," Reno Evening Gazette, p. 2, Jan. 23, 1962.
"Historical McGill Nevada – Smelter," facebook.com.
"History of Gambling in Wendover," eveleth.tripod.com.
"History of Glenbrook, Nevada," glenbrooklaketahoenv.com.
James, Susan. "In Virginia City, a lode of Comstock lore," latimes.com, Aug. 31, 2003.
James, Susan. "Short History of the Fourth Ward School," fourthwardschool.org.
"Joe Conforte," Reno Gazette-Journal, p. 18A, Nov. 14, 1986.
"Kennecott Nevada Mines Division," utahrails.net.
"Kimberly & Veteran," nvexpeditions.com.
"Kings Canyon Road, Carson City, Carson City, NV," Library of Congress, loc.gov.
"Lahontan Valley News and Fallon Eagle Standard," mondotimes.com.
"License Granted Copenhagen Bar," Nevada State Journal, p. 4, Jan. 15, 1935.
"The Lincoln Highway in Nevada," National Register of Historic Places Multiple Property Documentation Form, dot.nv.gov.
"Lincoln Highway Route, Road Conditions, and Directions," Packard Motor Co., Detroit, 1913.
Lynch, W.H. and Stewart, H.E. "Lincoln Highway From Fallon East Given Complete Survey," Reno Evening Gazette, p. 2, July 29, 1916.
"Maine Street Historic District," National Register of Historic Places Registration Form, shpo.nv.gov.
"The McGill Clubhouse," mcgillclubhouse.com.

"Middlegate," forgottennevada.org.

"Middlegate Station," atlasobscura.com.

"More than just a hostelry, it was a beacon before fire destroyed it 90 years ago today," nevadaappeal.com, Dec. 9, 2004.

Moreno, Richard. "Roadside History of Nevada," Mountain Press Publishing Co., Missuola, Mont., 2000.

"Motor Vehicle Registrations By State," fhwa.dot.gov.

"National Register #87000714, Kitzmeyer Furniture Factory," noehill.com.

"National Register of Historic Places in Eureka County," noehill.com.

"National Register of Historic Places Multiple Property Documentation Form, OMB 1024-0018" (Nevada fire stations), shpo.nv.gov.

"Nevada: Lahontan Dam and Power Station," nps.gov.

"Nevada Place Names Population 1860-2000," blackrockdesert.org.

"Nevada, United States," Museum of Gaming History, chipguide.themogh.org.

Newton, Marilyn. "Nevada's Hazen noted for notorious hanging," rgj.com, Aug. 29, 2014.

Newton, Marilyn and MacDonald, Douglas. "Financier slept on town flag," Reno Evening Gazette, Entertainment, p. 4, April 7, 1972.

Oberding, Janice. "Ghosts and Legends of Nevada's Highway 50," Haunted America, 2018.

Oliver, William E. "Pilgrimage on Wheels," Utah Historical Quarterly, Vol. 32, No. 1, 1964.

"Park Motel and Park Grocery," 4thprater.onlinenevada.org.

"Paul Laxalt State Building," sierranevadageotourism.org.

Peterson, Jesse G. "The Lincoln Highway and Its Changing Routes in Utah," Utah Historical Quarterly, Vol. 69, No. 3, Nov. 3, 2001.

Picon, Ed. "Three Nevada Gates," nevadagram.com.

"Pioneer Resident of Austin Dies at Oakland," Reno Evening Gazette, p. 7, July 14, 1939.

Pitsenberger, Trey and Monica. "Following the Lincoln Highway at Zephyr Cove, Nevada," pitsenberger.com, June 23, 2021.

Provost, Stephen H. "Carson City Century," Century Cities Publishing, 2022.

"Ragtown (Leeteville)," nvexpeditions.com.

"Raine's Market," rainesmarket.com.

"Riepetown," onlinenevada.org.

"Riepetown Nevada History and Photos," members.nbci.com.

Rocha, Guy. "Origin of Fernley's Name Shrouded in Mystery," cityoffernley.org.

"Ruth," nvexpeditions.com.

"Selz, Schwab & Co.," encyclopedia.chicagohistory.

Shamberger, Hugh A. "The Story of Fairview, Churchill County, Nevada," United States, 1973.

"The Shoe Tree of Middlegate," travelnevada.com.

"Sparks," onlinenevada.org.

"Sparks," shpo.nv.gov.

"Sparks, Nevada Roundhouse Panorama," cprr.org.

"St. Charles Hotel," consonpedia.com.

"Stagecoach, Nevada: Cactus Building," roadsideamerica.com.

"Steamboat," nvexpeditions.com.

"Stillwater," nvexpeditions.com.

"Stillwater School," ccmuseumomeka.net.

"U.S. 40 Begins (1929-1945)," 4thprater.onlinenevada.org.

"Tahoe Biltmore History," tahoebiltmore.com.

"Tahoe Resorts Busy As Preparations Are Made For Summer Season Opening," Nevada State Journal, p. 9, May 19, 1940.
"These Healing Hot Springs In Nevada Have A Truly Fascinating History," onlyinyourstate.com, Feb. 5, 2022.
"The Twisted Story Behind Nevada's Bowers Mansion," theculturetrip.com.
"Victory Highway in Nevada MPDF," dot.nv.gov.
"Wadsworth," nvexpeditions.com.
"Washoe Club's Haunted History," travelchannel.com.
"The Washoe Club History," thewashoeclubmuseum.com.
"Westgate," forgottennevada.org.
"White Pine is Proud of Having State's Oldest Elected Officer," Nevada State Journal, p. 9, Dec. 15, 1957.
"The Winters' Ranch (Rancho Del Sierra)," nv-landmarks.com.

The remains of Pinto House, mentioned in early travel guides. It's about seven miles east of Eureka on the south side of U.S. 50. *Author photo*

About the author

Stephen H. Provost has written several books about life in 20th century America. This is his sixth book on America's highways. During more than three decades in journalism, he has worked as a managing editor, copy desk chief, columnist and reporter at five newspapers. Now a full-time author, he has written on such diverse topics as dragons, mutant superheroes, mythic archetypes, language, department stores and his hometown. Visit him online and read his blogs at stephenhprovost.com.

Did you enjoy this book?

Recommend it to a friend. And please consider rating it and/or leaving a brief review online at Amazon, Barnes & Noble and Goodreads.

STEPHEN H. PROVOST

Also by the author

Works of Fiction

The Talismans of Time (Academy of the Lost Labyrinth, Book 1)
Pathfinder of Destiny (Academy of the Lost Labyrinth, Book 2)
Astral Academy
Memortality (The Memortality Saga, Book 1)
Paralucidity (The Memortality Saga, Book 2)
The Only Dragon
Identity Break
Feathercap
Nightmare's Eve

Works of Nonfiction

Yesterday's Highways
America's First Highways
Highway 99: The History of California's Main Street
Highway 101: The History of El Camino Real
Highways of the South
The Lincoln Highway in California (with Gary Kinst)
The Great American Shopping Experience
Martinsville Memories
Fresno Growing Up
The Century Cities series:
    Cambria Century, Carson City Century,
    Charleston Century, Danville Century,
    Fresno Century, Goldfield Century,
    Greensboro Century, Huntington Century,
    Roanoke Century, San Luis Obispo Century

Praise for other works

"If you have any interest in highways, old diners and motels and such, or 20th century US history, this book is for you. It is without a doubt one of the best highway books ever published."
— Dan R. Young, Highway 101 historian, on **Yesterday's Highways**

"Both books are well-researched, nicely written, and illustrated with good black and white photographs, and both contribute importantly to highway literature."
— Wayne Shannon, *Jefferson Highway Declaration*, on **Yesterday's Highways** and **America's First Highways**

"... an engaging narrative that pulls the reader into the story and onto the road. ... I highly recommend **Highway 99: The History of California's Main Street**, whether you're a roadside archaeology nut or just someone who enjoys a ripping story peppered with vintage photographs."
— Barbara Gossett, Society for Commercial Archaeology Journal

"Profusely illustrated throughout, **Highway 99** is unreservedly recommended as an essential and core addition to every community and academic library's California History collections."
— California Bookwatch

"... it contains a lot of information I hadn't heard before. Both books prove well-written with few weaknesses..."
— Ron Warnick, route66news.com, on **Yesterday's Highways** and **America's First Highways**

"An essential primer for anyone seeking an entrée into the genre. Provost serves up a smorgasbord of highlights gleaned from his personal memories of and research into the various nooks and crannies of what 'used-to-be' in professional team sports."
— Tim Hanlon, Good Seats Still Available, on **A Whole Different League**

"As informed and informative as it is entertaining and absorbing, **Fresno Growing Up** is very highly recommended for personal, community, and academic library 20th Century
American History collections."

— John Burroughs, Reviewer's Bookwatch

"The complex idea of mixing morality and mortality is a fresh twist on the human condition. ... **Memortality** is one of those books that will incite more questions than it answers. And for fandom, that's a good thing."

— Ricky L. Brown, Amazing Stories

"Punchy and fast paced, **Memortality** reads like a graphic novel. ... (Provost's) style makes the trippy landscapes and mind-bending plot points more believable and adds a thrilling edge to this vivid crossover fantasy."

— Foreword Reviews

"The genres in this volume span horror, fantasy, and science-fiction, and each is handled deftly. ... **Nightmare's Eve** should be on your reading list. The stories are at the intersection of nightmare and lucid dreaming, up ahead a signpost ... next stop, your reading pile. Keep the nightlight on."

— R.B. Payne, Cemetery Dance

"**Memortality** by Stephen Provost is a highly original, thrilling novel unlike anything else out there." — David McAfee, bestselling author of

33 A.D., 61 A.D., and *79 A.D.*

"Provost sticks mostly to the classics: vampires, ghosts, aliens, and even dragons. But trekking familiar terrain allows the author to subvert readers' expectations. ... Provost's poetry skillfully displays the same somber themes as the stories. ... Worthy tales that prove external forces are no more terrifying than what's inside people's heads."

— Kirkus Reviews on **Nightmare's Eve**

"The story feels so close, so intimate, we as readers experience the emotions, the events, and the conflicts, in what feels like real time. Gut-wrenchingly so."

— Stephen Mark Rainey, author of *Blue Devil Island,* on **Death's Doorstep**

AMERICA'S LONELIEST ROAD

Continue the journey...

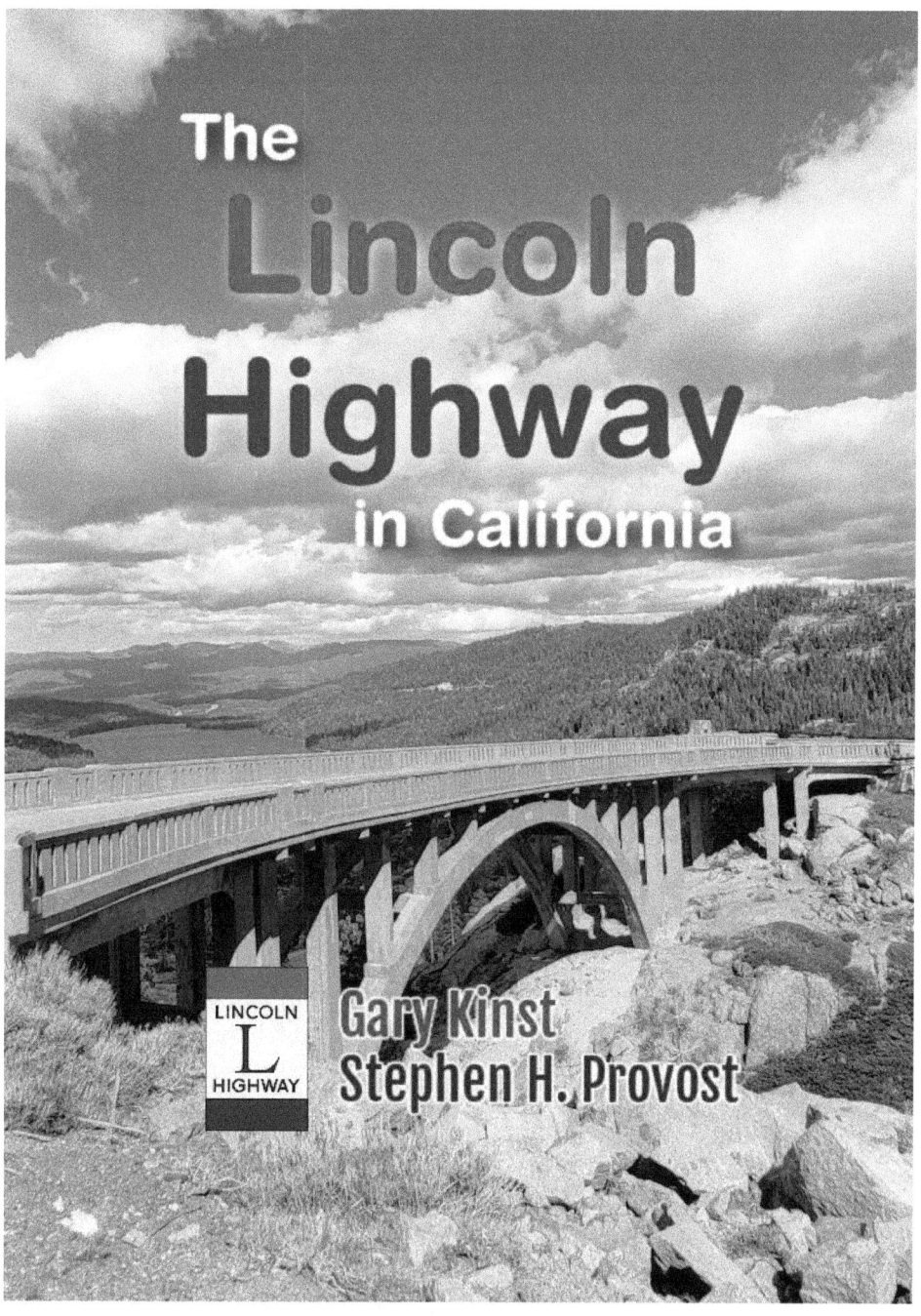

Now that you've followed the Lincoln Highway in Nevada, keep going with this comprehensive historical travel guide to the Lincoln Highway in California. Fall 2022